Praise for *Sons of the Eastern Plains*

This colorful, soul-written, unforgettable account of Lanny Cook's life, his family and special friends, captures the reader's heart with spontaneous laughter and tear. A magical introspection, this candid disclosure of one's relationship with Jesus Christ moves the reader with an undeniable force, leaving a sanctifying reverie. Each chapter is punctuated with tugging poetry by Clarice Cook. I'm honored to know the Cooks, and to be an integral part of the lives of these true-blooded Americans. It's a compelling read.

—Bob Serrao
Minister and author

You will absolutely love this book. Lanny Cook's tales of his childhood growing up in rural Colorado will make you laugh; his account of the loss of a close friend will cause you to pause and consider the brevity of life; and his spiritual journey will provoke you to search for life's meaning and purpose. Rarely does a single book take you through such a powerful range of emotion and feeling. This is an important read.

—Gary M. Beasley
Pastor; author of *The Conquering Church, The Complete Family,* and *Complete Evangelism*

Sons of the Eastern Plains pulled and tugged at every heart string in my body. I laughed out loud, wept to myself, and felt the rush of adrenaline almost as if I were a part of Lanny's adventures. If you enjoy a cacophony of emotions in your reading material, you will not be disappointed as I highly recommend Lanny's latest work.

—Reverend David Baca
The Crossing Church of the Nazarene, Westminster CO

This is Norman Rockwell, *Leave it to Beaver, Dennis the Menace* and *Little House on the Prairie* all rolled into one! Extremely entertaining and a joy to read.

It's refreshing to read a story that comes from the memories of one who is thankful for the life he has been given and the people he holds dear to his heart. It's written honestly, bringing back to mind what families should be. The inclusion of his moms' poetry is a gift to the reader, from the heart of a mother who treasured those she loved. Lanny's reflections on the Word of God woven through his story shed new and inspiring light on well-known Scriptures, exciting me once again for what I know is coming and what the purpose of life really is.

—Jennifer Strauch
Actor and writer, Faith on Stage

Sons of the Eastern Plains by Dr. Lanny Cook is a breath of fresh air! When Dr. Cook takes you on a journey of his childhood and experiences, you can't help but to reflect on your own. This book shares a genuine all-American "Andy Griffith" nostalgia feel with the turn of each page. This is the first book I have read that offered me such an eclectic collection of emotion; from one moment to the next I went from crying to laughing exuberantly. So refreshing!

—Regina Baca
Stephen Leader for Stephen Ministries,
The Crossing Church of the Nazarene

Dr. Lanny Cook presents a masterful offering of his life adventure. He bookends his colorful journey of childhood through adult relationships and eye-widening events, with the most spiritually intimate experience in the life of a believer in Jesus Christ. These precious moments demonstrate the title of his book so very tenderly. To have the opportunity to experience them as Lanny did will leave you changed. Between these precious bookends, you will enjoy the flavors, colors, and imagery of his detailed word pictures, poetry, and prose.

—Steven Nuss
Licensed professional counselor and
certified addiction counselor

SONS *of the* EASTERN PLAINS: *A Memoir*

SONS *of the* EASTERN PLAINS: *A Memoir*

Lanny K. Cook

Deep River Books

Published by
Deep River Books
Sisters, Oregon
www.deepriverbooks.com

Unless otherwise indicated the original poetry contained within this work was written by Clarice D. Cook (Mom) and is used with permission. ("Buddies Forever!" and excerpts from "Painting Butterflies for You!").

ISBN: 9781940269511

Library of Congress: 2015938005

Printed in the USA

Cover design by Joe Bailen, Contajus Designs

Dedication

To my cousin, Timothy Eugene Trusty along with the many other loved ones who have gone on to find rest in the eternal hope of our Lord and Savior, Jesus Christ.

Contents

Acknowledgments

I am forever grateful to the God of my fathers, Who has blessed my life with an amazing family and wonderful friends, my wife, Debbie, my parents, Gordon and Clarice, my sons, Brian and Dennis, my brothers Randy and Danny, my amazing grandchildren, nieces and nephews, along with those special friends who make up my extended family of faith. My life has truly been blessed. All of you have touched me, and I have grown. Nothing in life is more valuable than family and special friends. Thank you all, for your encouragement and support!

Psalm 139:1-10 NASB

God's Omnipresence and Omniscience.
For the choir director. A Psalm of David.

139 O LORD, You have searched me and known me.

2 You know when I sit down and when I rise up;
You understand my thought from afar.

3 You scrutinize my path and my lying down,
And are intimately acquainted with all my ways.

4 Even before there is a word on my tongue,
Behold, O LORD, You know it all.

5 You have enclosed me behind and before,
And laid Your hand upon me.

6 Such knowledge is too wonderful for me;
It is too high, I cannot attain to it.

7 Where can I go from Your Spirit?
Or where can I flee from Your presence?

8 If I ascend to heaven, You are there;
If I make my bed in Sheol, behold, You are there.

9 If I take the wings of the dawn,
If I dwell in the remotest part of the sea,

10 Even there Your hand will lead me,
And Your right hand will lay hold of me.

A Word From The Author

As we grow older, it's amazing how time seems to fly. My grandparents regularly mentioned this phenomenon by saying, "Where has the time gone?" As a child, I never understood, but as I have grown older, and as my children have grown and the grandkids continue to grow, I am amazed as how time flies by at an increasingly rapid pace.

There is no avoiding life's reality that we are born, live for a specific amount of time, and, then sadly, are destined to die. As we grow older, most folks begin to ponder life's biggest question, "What lies beyond this world?" From history's beginning, humanity has diligently sought the answer to this one elusive question. Ancient civilizations created their own religious systems to address mankind's innate desire for eternal significance and devised belief systems that tried to provide hope amid the reality of death. The Egyptians, Greeks, and Romans worshipped a multitude of gods, and created religions that elevated leaders to equality with their gods in an attempt to secure their position in the next life.

I have attended many funeral services where the minister spoke about the *dash between the moments of birth and death*. They allude to the fact that this dash represents a life that, in many cases, spans decades and, in some situations, nearly a century. The dash belies the fact that every life is marked by joy, peace, happiness, adversity, challenges, and trials. Each dash is as unique as the person who lies beneath a particular headstone. Each dash represents a lifetime of dreams, ambitions, disappointments, and victories.

Growing up, I always tried to live by the motto, "It's not what you get out of life that's important, but rather, what you put into life that defines one's contribution to a life well-spent." The story that follows is an example of actual events that are represented by the dash between dates. It's the story of life; its jubilations, and its tragedies. It's a story, taken from some experiences within the dashes of my own existence; especially from those of my childhood where the foundation of hope, security, and faith were instilled into the essence of my life by the determined efforts of my parents.

The importance of providing children with a stable, secure childhood cannot be overstated. In most cases, childhood experiences will make or break an individual's ability to overcome the obstacles and challenges they encounter along the way. After spending twenty-eight years in the public school system as a teacher and as an administrator, I saw first-hand the impact of the relationships, experiences, and circumstances that were placed upon the students I encountered. In some cases, these young people completely overcame circumstances. In other cases, I witnessed how an inability to overcome early life circumstances crippled and hindered these individuals from enjoying a fulfilling and prosperous life.

I was blessed to grow up in a loving, stable, secure, functioning home on the eastern plains of Colorado. I was raised in Denver, but the small town of Snyder, in Morgan County, was the home of my grandparents. The eastern plains of Colorado provided the backdrop for the adventures that transformed me from a child, into a man. Colorado's eastern plains will always be home, at least in my heart. Our home made all the difference as it prepared me to venture out into the world. It not only provided me with the foundation for success, but it also provided a belief system that has helped me overcome all of life's challenges. These pages contain stories of events as I perceived them. I pray that as you read this story, your heart may be touched by your own childhood memories. And as you reflect on your own days of frolicking through your childhood, I hope your own fun-filled adventures of days in the sun will unfold before you.

> "Train up a child in the way he should go: and when he is old, he will not depart from it."
>
> —Proverbs 22:6 KJV

CHAPTER 1

A Life Well-Spent

As I near the sixth decade on this Earth, I reflect back on specific events that left a lasting impact on my life. Numerous events are forever etched in my mind. I remember exactly what happened: where I was; who I was with; and what I was doing. Several of those include the day President John F. Kennedy was assassinated, the time when astronaut John Glenn first orbited the Earth in the Mercury capsule, and the day the Apollo 1 capsule caught fire on the launch pad, killing three astronauts, Roger B. Chaffee, Ed White and Gus Grissom. I also remember the day the Challenger Space Shuttle exploded, the day Elvis Presley died, the days when Martin Luther King and Robert Kennedy were both assassinated, the day Princess Diana was killed in a car crash, and the day terror came to America on September 11, 2001.

All of these notable headlines left a lasting impression on my mind and on my heart. But other experiences impacted me in a profound, deeper, and more personal way. One of the most significant relationships that I've enjoyed provides foundational insight into the rest of this story and contains one of those moments that is forever ingrained in my heart and mind. It happened just a few years ago, and it involved two dear friends that I had known all of my adult life.

Les and Mary were pillars within the community where I grew up. Les was the principal of the local high school and would later move into administration as superintendent of the district schools. Les hired me for my first teaching job when he served as the director of human services for the schools.

I became closely acquainted with Les and Mary through the Methodist church when I became a member of the congregation. They were both charter members of the local congregation and served in all sorts of leadership roles within the church. When I joined the choir, as a bass singer, I had the pleasure of sitting next to Les every week at practice and every Sunday in church. We became extremely close friends in spite of the 40-year age difference. In many ways, we were kindred-spirits and both enjoyed a good laugh as well as great conversation. Les and Mary's story would have made a great book in itself and, as I drew closer to them, I became intrigued and amazed at the huge repertoire of life experiences and adventures they were always willing to share.

Mary was born in England and Les was born in Connecticut back in the early 20th century. Mary lived the first 22 years of her life in England. As a young woman, she held a secretarial position at the Winchester War Office during World War II. Part of her duties included writing letters to the next of kin for soldiers who had been killed or who were missing in action. One of the most difficult tasks she was ever required to do was to help notify the families of an entire regiment that had been lost near Singapore. I believe that these experiences were instrumental in developing her life-long commitment to serve others through acts of kindness and giving.

Les grew up in an age when hard work was considered essential. He was a teenager toward the end of the Great Depression, and he learned at an early age that you can't take things for granted. The only way to survive was through diligent effort and preparation.

After graduating from high school, Les made his way to Colorado from Connecticut to work on a degree at the Colorado School of Agriculture, which is now Colorado State University. Upon completing his degree, World War II broke out and Les chose to volunteer. His eyesight almost kept him out of the service, but the doctor asked him if he wanted in or wanted out. Les adamantly declared he wanted to serve his country. Even though he had a degree, he entered as an enlisted man and became a corpsman, a battlefield medic. During the war he saw action in North Africa, Italy, and, in 1944, he was in the second wave of assault at the Normandy invasion. During his time in the Army, he obtained the rank of tech sergeant and was awarded numerous commendations, several battle or campaign stars, two Bronze Stars, a Purple Heart, and the Army Soldier's Medal. In those few short years, he witnessed firsthand more death, destruction, and heart-wrenching misery than most people see in a lifetime.

Mary and Les met during World War II while he was stationed in England, and after finally agreeing to go out with him, which was probably in part to his being a young, good-looking American soldier with a consistent ration of cigarettes, she fell for him. Two days before he was to leave for the Invasion of Normandy, Les went AWOL (Away Without Official Leave) in order to propose. After she said, "Yes," he had to hurry back to the encampment before it was discovered that he was missing. Apparently the Lord was keeping an eye on him, because he was able to hitch a ride back to his station from a British lieutenant before anyone realized he was out on his own. It's a good thing that the invasion didn't begin two days earlier; Mary might have had to marry him in the brig, but at least then she would have known where he was and that he was safe and sound.

The two were supposed to get married in England, but Les was shipped back to the states before Mary could get him to officially say, "I do." So, after the war she followed him back to America in order to make Les stand true to his word. It took Mary some time to complete all of the paperwork necessary to enter this country, but, when she finally made it to the states, instead of being met by Les in New York on November 11, 1946, she was greeted by Les' brother Phillip and his wife, Beatrice. It seems that Les had made his way to Colorado in order to start a master's degree program.

Mary ended up spending a short time with Les' parents in Connecticut before boarding a train and making her way to Colorado. Mary loved to tell the story of her adventure to nab Les. When she stayed with Les's parents for that short period of time, his mom tried to talk her into marrying his brother Lou. After all, Lou was a lot more stable than his brother and would make a better husband, but Mary would have nothing to do with that. She was in love with Les. She made her way out to the Wild West and the two were married on November 26, 1946, in Loveland, Colorado. Former Vice President

Hubert Humphrey once said that "behind every successful man is a surprised mother-in-law." In this case, I think it might have been Les' mom who was surprised that the marriage actually took.

Mary was truly one of a kind. I have never met anyone quite like her, and I know I never will again. There are not enough adjectives in the English language to describe Mary's unique and remarkable characteristics. Just the fact that she left her native country of England to venture into an unknown world in pursuit of the love of her life, is a testament to this amazing woman's character. Courageous, adventuresome, tenacious, independent, determined, brave, tough, caring, confident, wise, insightful, dignified, resourceful, giving, loving, and a great friend are all words that could describe Mary.

Tom Brokaw's book, *"The Greatest Generation,"* was filled with stories of individuals like Les and Mary. In my mind, I know that this amazing couple was truly one of the greatest of their generation. As John F. Kennedy proclaimed in his inaugural address,

> "The torch has been passed to a new generation of Americans, born in this century, tempered by war, disciplined by a hard and bitter peace, proud of our ancient heritage and unwilling to witness or permit the slow undoing of those human rights to which this nation has always been committed . . ."

Les and Mary were living examples of this profound declaration. They both possessed the characteristics of being adventurers. Modern-day explorers and a true pioneer couple of the 20th century. Mary dared to step out of her comfort zone to chase after a dream. She left her homeland for a lifelong adventure that took her all over the world. But the courage she must have had to leave England to start a new life in a strange and distant land is beyond my comprehension. Maybe it was courage, but then again, maybe it was just being head-over-heels in love with a man named Lester.

Mary came to this country willingly and enthusiastically. She was as proud of her American citizenship as she was her English heritage. I always thought it fitting that she celebrated her birthday on June 14, the day our nation celebrates Flag Day. Even though you could always detect that English accent in her voice, Mary was as much of an American as any who were born in this country.

Through the years Les and Mary traveled together all over the world. Mary traveled to forty-four different countries throughout her lifetime and Les had another half-dozen or so that he could include in his repertoire of world travels. Together, they volunteered for a two-year stint with the Peace Corp on a little island called Tonga. When Mary would share stories about their adventures, I couldn't help but admire their ability to leave the comforts of home to help others in a third-world country. I remember hearing a recording that they had brought back from their time in Tonga. It was of the choir from the church they attended. What an amazing rendition of the Hallelujah Chorus sung a cappella.

Les and Mary spent a lifetime making a difference in the lives of those they encountered. Mary came to this country to chase after a dream, but in the process, along with Les, she made a difference in the lives of more people than anyone could ever imagine. When she crossed the big pond, I'm sure she had no idea the legacy that she would leave with Les right by her side.

I have said that Les could be considered the prime minister of the local school district, and if Les was the prime minister, then Mary was *the queen*. Many folks in the school district administration commonly referred to her as "Queen Mary." I would affectionately call her "Queen Mum." A title that she earned out of deep respect for the great individual that she was! Through the years, Les became one of my closest friends, mentors, and confidants, while Mary evolved into what I referred to as "my second mom." Affectionately, she would always introduce me as "her number-two son," even though we shared no known blood lines. However, being informally adopted into her life brought me great pleasure and was a humbling honor.

Les and Mary were founding members of the local Methodist church, where they actively served on nearly every committee possible. They were a pillar on which their church was built and on which it has continued to survive. They were a couple of unwavering faith, along with deep integrity, of direct and sometimes blatant honesty, as well as individuals of profound character. Mary in particular could keep everyone in stitches. She had a Brit's sense of humor and she was quite the story teller and jokester. She could tell a joke with the best of them. Her zest for life was a light that endeared her to everyone she met, and Les' wisdom and common sense made him one of the best mentors and friends that I ever encountered.

When Mary was in her early eighties, she lost her sight and was faced with living the rest of her life with indistinct and totally blurred vision. However, she continued on with her usual zest and zeal, touching people in her typical, humorously profound way. She had the knack of making friends with just a single encounter, and, through her blindness as well as the other ailments that she endured, she reached out and touched the lives of everyone she met, including her nurses and doctors. I used to tell Mary when I would see her, "It's good to see you!" She would always come back with the same humorous retort, "I wish I could say the same!"

Mary had been diagnosed with mouth cancer, and she had been enduring radiation treatments for several weeks. My wife, Debbie, and I were preparing to head out on a weekend excursion with my son Dennis and his family. We had decided to head up to a place in Wyoming called Lake Hattie, which is about a three hour drive from Denver. It is a beautiful place just west of Laramie, lying within a valley, nestled within a majestic backdrop of snow-capped mountains. Before we left, I wanted to check in with Mary to let her and Les know we'd be out of town for the weekend, but would be back in town by Monday. During our conversation, Mary shared with me that she was having excruciating pain from radiation treatments. Knowing her as well as I did, I was surprised by her admission of any pain, since she had never complained of any physical ailment before, at least to me. She confided that she was dreading the next treatment which was scheduled to take place on Monday morning, since she didn't know how much more of this she could endure. Before ending our conversation, I assured her that we would come to visit her as soon as we got back from the lake.

We had an amazing time at the lake. There is something special, almost spiritual with spending time in the great outdoors, enjoying time with family and friends. And, when the time is spent with the grandkids too, it makes the time even more remarkable. I have a friend that always put it this way; "You love your kids, but you fall in love with your grandkids." I must admit that there is more truth to that saying than a rational adult would like to admit. So, spending time relaxing with the family, skipping rocks, fishing, walking the dogs, making S'mores around the campfire, and just basking in the sun create memories that last a lifetime.

When we woke up Monday morning, the weather had turned dreary and cold. Rather than hanging around to endure the possibility of yet another weather change, we decided it was time to pack up camp and head home. Dennis and his family decided to follow suit and before you knew it, the camp was torn down and we were headed back to Denver. As soon as we crossed into Colorado, I received a voice mail message on my cell phone which said, "If you want to see Mary, you need to get to the hospital right away." Immediately, I called to find out what was going on. I was told that Les had taken Mary to the hospital for another radiation treatment, and while there, she lost consciousness and lapsed into a coma. Apparently, she was waiting at death's door, and there was little hope that she would last much longer.

The next hour and a half flew by. I drove as fast I dared in an effort to get home, and drop off the pickup and camper before heading over to the hospital. Throughout the entire trip, my mind swirled around the thoughts about what had transpired in just a few short days. Why, it had been just four days earlier when I ended my conversation with Mary with our usual, "I love you," and "I'll see you soon!" I had no idea when I left for the weekend that this experience awaited me when I arrived home. Never could I have imagined that I would never have another conversation with the one that I referred to as "my number two Mom." The rainy, dreary weather, with the low-lying clouds seemed to accentuate the dream-like fog that whirled in my head at that moment in time.

Walking into the hospital, my mind was flooded with experiences from my past. I had this overwhelming sense of Déjà vu — I had walked this path before. When we walked into the hospital room, Les and two of their friends were standing at the foot of the bed where Mary was lying. On each side of the bed near her head, two nurses closely monitored a myriad of electronic devices that displayed her vital signs. When we walked into the room, Mary's appearance stunned me, although I tried not to let anyone see my reaction to the unexpected horror of how she looked. The radiation treatments had totally discolored the lower half of her face to the point of her being almost unrecognizable. I was shocked by the extent of her physical decline, which seemed to happen almost overnight.

I announced our arrival with a soft, "Hello." Mary, who was lying with the bed slightly elevated in an almost sitting position, instantly lifted up her arm, reaching out toward us as we walked up to her. Knowing that she had slipped into a coma, I was a bit surprised by her movement. As we drew close to her, and in my mind, I felt quite satisfied that she had responded to my voice. I grabbed her hand that was lying by her side, before softly saying, "Hi Mary, it's Lanny and Debbie, we've come to see you." There was no response to us as she continued to reach her left arm out toward the ceiling of the room.

Instantly, I knew that she wasn't responding to my voice. She was reaching out to eternity. Mary's eyes had been opened, her earthly blindness removed, and she was now able to see past the veil of earthly boundaries. She was reaching beyond the constraints of this life, into the spiritual realm that leads to eternal life. Mary was reaching for her Lord and Savior, who was there to take her home. For the first time in more than ten years, her physical eyes opened to see the Light. I stood there in awe for a moment, knowing that she was looking past the confines of her mortality, seeing first-hand the beauty and the wonders of God's eternity. I realized that I was standing in the presence of Jesus, the One whom Mary had lived her life in service to, and the One to whom she was now reaching. In but a moment, she took one last breath, her arm fell back to her side, and she closed her eyes in death as the monitors became silent.

Les gave her one last, tender kiss on the cheek as he tenderly caressed her weather-worn hand. He then turned to me, and said, "She would appreciate if you give her a kiss goodbye." I leaned in as I gently kissed her still warm, lifeless forehead. "Goodbye Mum," I whispered as the five of us gathered around her for our final farewell. We held hands as I began to pray out loud, thanking God for this wonderful lady who had such a profound impact on our lives. We praised Him for allowing her to have a long, productive life and for the legacy she had left behind in each of us, as well as in the multitude of friends and family. I thanked God for taking her so peacefully, even though it was so unexpected, in spite of her battle with this treacherous and deadly disease.

When we opened our eyes from prayer, we were greeted with the most amazing sight that I have ever witnessed. Even though it was a cloudy, dreary, gloomy day, when we opened our eyes, we were engulfed with the most intense golden rays of sunlight that I had ever seen in my life. Somehow, the setting sun had broken through the clouds, permeated the half-open blinds on the windows and filled the entire room with a brilliant, magnificent golden radiance. It was like the doors of heaven had opened to allow Mary to enter in to her eternal glory. On the night that Mary left this Earth and ascended into the heavens to be with her Lord and Master, I can only imagine that she was greeted by a heavenly host of angels singing the Hallelujah Chorus. I was certain that we had just experienced that blessed moment, and Mary entered into heaven singing right along at the top of her lungs. Mary's faith had seen her through this life and, as promised, it carried her through the door that leads to life everlasting.

Certain moments prompt reflection on the important questions of life's significance, such as, "Why are we here? What is our purpose? Is there life after this one?" The birth of a child, a wedding, a baptism, graduations and, of course, the death of a loved one, all lend themselves to ponder those big-picture questions. Life is a journey, a trek that takes us through some daunting challenges and trials, taking us to a place that none of us could ever imagine when we first start out on this adventure. Les confided with me that evening that he wasn't prepared to let Mary go that day. When the day started out, there was nothing that would indicate this would be her last day on Earth. None of us are ever prepared for moments such as this, even when we've been given plenty of notice. There's always something else to be done, something else to be said, or one last thing we intended to do for those we love before they go on to this next journey.

As we left the hospital that evening, leaving Mary's body behind, my mind swirled with thoughts of both my past and the present. A multitude of questions entered my mind about the circumstances of Mary's passing from this life into the next. For the next several days, my mind was constantly flooded with memories—memories about Mary—memories revolving around those unforgettable moments in life that had molded me into the person that I had become. Moments that had so deeply impacted my life that they were forever etched in my mind. Mary's passing brought to the forefront of my mind many of the most significant moments of my life, and as a result, in my mind, I was carried back to the days of my childhood. Losing a loved one causes us to reflect on the past, while pondering what lies ahead in the future.

Mary's passing was a poignant reminder of the frailty of this life. Through it all, I was reminded of a similar experience, one that I had encountered nearly thirty years earlier. Actually, one that culminated three decades earlier, but actually began with my first recollections in life. It was the journey of my childhood and my relationship with my cousin, Tim—probably the closest friend that I have ever had. Times such as this one always cause me to reflect on the most precious of memories: the places I've been, the people I've met, the roads that I've traveled; memories of my childhood, and memories of those I've loved the most. Ah, memories. Yes, precious memories, how they linger, and oh, how they touch the deepest recesses of the soul.

The Wings of the Dawn

The "Wings of the Dawn," what a beautiful phrase,
Evoking an image, 'midst the sweetest of days.
Like an eagle in flight, upon outstretched wings,
Soaring high in the sky, above pastoral scenes.
Beyond the clouds, not hindered by weather,
God's Spirit of love draws His children together.
The horizon is tranquil, engulfed in the Light,
It beckons us near—toward a beautiful sight.

The future we see . . . it's almost in reach,
Like waves gently lapping on the sand of a beach.
Scenes that appear as we've soared through this life,
Are sprinkled with joy, with some trials and strife.
The Word that is shared holds a message so clear,
We must silence our heart, in an effort to hear;
Each verse is quite different, as the seasons fly by,
We hear a new message, as the midnight draws nigh.
For the time fast approaches, when we will sail no more,
To an earthly adventure, toward a beckoning shore;
So we must lift up our eyes toward the Glory above,
Where lives are united in God's boundless love!

A hand lifts us up as the wind under wing,
Sweet rhapsodies ring out as a fresh gentle spring.
Salvation He offers—We will wander no more,
Now glide through the heavens—His Way to explore.
We fly toward the entrance—to the door high above,
That welcomes our presence to abide in His love.
And there we will enter on the "Wings of the Dawn,"
Within the Glory of heaven, our souls will live on!

—Lanny K. Cook

CHAPTER 2

Trails From a Distant Path

My earliest memories intertwine with those of my cousin, Tim. From the day he was released from the hospital, we were together. Tim's mom, Aunt Dorothy, was Dad's sister, but Mom and Dad were more like best friends with Dorothy and Uncle Don. We were always going places and doing things together. I think that Uncle Don became the brother that my Dad never had. Actually, they were closer than brothers. Dad and Uncle Don had worked the oil rigs together before Tim and I were born, and Uncle Don fit the rugged John Wayne mold of the typical oil rigger. Only Don was a lot more interesting than "the Duke."

Dad was smaller than Don but had as much fight and determination as anyone I've ever known. There wasn't anything Dad couldn't do once he set his mind to it. They were both from the working class of society. Both worked hard and long for every advantage the world could afford them. Neither one received any handouts as they fought to provide their families with the conveniences available in modern America. Frequently, they both worked two jobs in order to pay the bills. They were examples of how honesty, integrity, commitment, and hard work rewards you for hard labor. They lived by example, showing us how to live life to its fullest while being responsible for our actions.

To look at Dad you'd think that his blood line came from Indian heritage, and as children, all of us took pride in the possibility that Native American blood might run through our veins. There was never any proof of that, but it was possible since there were some French-Canadian ancestors in our bloodlines. After all, it was a common practice for many of the French settlers to marry an Indian maiden while venturing out into the wild. A culminating curiosity was the fact that on great, great Grandpa Henry Cook's death certificate, his mother's race was listed as unknown, while my Grandpa Cook always refused to discuss genetic links to his past. Even though there was a reluctance to discuss his ancestry, traces within the family display a distinct Native American resemblance. However, over the years, additional evidence might lead us to believe that there really isn't any Native American blood coursing through our veins, but instead, it is more likely that the blood line that our grandparents refused to talk about had come from the Abrahamic lineage, in other words, the Jewish contingent.

Regardless, interest in our heritage aroused our curiosity about where our forefathers originated. The stories we heard as we were growing up allowed us to gain a deep appreciation for who we were and where we'd come from. These stories helped to shape and mold us into who we would become. Family folklore passed down from generation to generation, told over and over again, became ingrained in our minds and our imaginations. These tales of family lore stirred the imagination of a child, while providing a hope, or, maybe I should say, a biased speculation, that there may have actually been a bit of Indian heritage associated with the unknown genetic links from the distant paths.

Since the ranch that Grandpa Cook homesteaded had once been alive and bustling with the lives and activities of long-forgotten native tribes, probably from the Cheyenne, Arapahoe, and Ute people, we thrilled to the stories of finding rare artifacts and arrowheads that littered the sandy hills surrounding the ranch house and the outbuildings. Stories of artifacts that lay buried for a hundred years or more beneath the dry, parched prairie sand. Artifacts that would be exposed by the harsh winds and weather of the region, allowing them to be discovered like a lost treasure by anyone lucky enough to stumble across them.

There were still piles of flint chippings scattered along the sides of those ancient hills, where once-proud braves patiently and skillfully chipped their knives, arrowheads, and spear-points. Scrapers crafted for tanning deer and buffalo hides resulted in unprecedented craftsmanship for using such primitive tools. These skills had been passed down for generations, talents that are all but lost through the assimilation of a people into modern society. On the dusty old hills of that ranch, remnants of fire rings stood as scattered monuments of a long-deserted Indian village, and a still-visible trail wound miles across the desolate, prairie grasses through ravines and gulches, to meet the South Platte River banks at the old cow-town of Snyder.

We were mesmerized by our parents and grandparents sharing stories of the Overland Trail, the infamous trail that stretched westward to a promised land from the east. The trail was still visible from the hill above the ranch house. There were thought-provoking stories of wagon trains and settlers who dreamed of brighter futures and land for homesteading as they labored forth on that dusty old trail. There were tales of pre-ranch life in the Denver-Arvada area where Grandpa Cook and his father worked at the ice house in the foothills of the Rocky Mountains, which allowed them to run their own ice business where deliveries were made to businesses and residents through the use of horse-drawn wagons and then later on by truck.

We listened intently to reminiscing about the "good ole days," of homesteading the 165-acre parcel on the parched, arid plains of northeastern Colorado, often referred to as "the dry-lands." Since Grandpa Cook, his brother Charlie and their father had all homesteaded neighboring parcels, listening to the stories of hardships associated with homesteading their own land was like experiencing history in action.

It was on the side of a sagebrush-covered hill, in a portion of the country referred to as the "badlands," named because of the rolling hills with deep ravines, that the homestead was claimed. A shelter was built, not too far from a natural spring where the sod "dugout" served as a makeshift home without the conveniences of electricity, running water, or indoor plumbing. Here in this raw, native land of natural grasses, my Grandpa Cook painstakingly raised Black Angus cattle while patiently coaxing the harsh, virgin land to yield the "dry-land" crop of winter wheat. It was truly the pioneering spirit that allowed him and his family to wring out of this relentless land not only a living, but a way of life.

There were hardships beyond imagination found on that barren prairie ranch. Rattlesnake migrations were common. The ground would crawl with thousands of poisonous reptiles, as they slithered their way to an unknown destination. Vivid descriptions of such hair-raising experiences would scare the liver out of the kids, causing everyone to take extra caution every time they stepped out the door of the ranch and onto the placid landscape surrounding the ranch. So we learned early on in life to always be on the look-out for those highly camouflaged, deadly vipers that lurked around the edges of the sage brush or rocky ledges. Actually, it never mattered whether there was a migration on or not, there was always an overabundance of snakes lurking around the outbuildings, probably in hopes of making a quick meal out of the mice that scampered throughout the barns, sheds and pump houses. Garter snakes, water snakes, diamondback rattlers and bull snakes that grew to lengths nearly six-feet long were native to this part of the country. Why, just the sight of them was enough to scare the bejeebers out of any youngster as they frolicked throughout the countryside.

Dad always told stories about how he used to carry a grapefruit-sized rock or two in his hands as he would walk out to the pastures to herd the cows home in the evenings. Like the biblical David, the rocks were his weapons of choice to be used against the dangerous reptiles that slithered through the sage, the buffalo grass and the prairie's yucca plants. Many times he would kill a maddened snake, which had been disturbed by his human presence, by throwing a rock with such force and accuracy that the creature didn't stand a chance. On more than one occasion, his faithful dog would get to the snake first; skillfully jousting with the poisonous serpent until the opportunity arose to lock its jaws behind the snake's head and relentlessly shake it until all signs of life were gone. Part of the ritual of killing a rattlesnake was to then place a rock or stick on its head, place your foot on the rock or stick and then pick up the snake by its tail to carefully pull off the rattles. As the Native Americans who had originally occupied this land centuries earlier, and whose shields were adorned with the bloody scalps of their foes, the dominance and victory over this parched land was celebrated as the rattles were plucked off this symbol of evil.

We heard stories about blinding dust storms that plagued the land during the dustbowl days. One storm put Dad in the hospital with dust pneumonia when he was sixteen. Many people died during severe dust storms that were common during the days of the Great Depression. Once the family was caught in a bad storm while driving home from town. The dust was so thick that Grandpa couldn't see the road. The whole family was on board and ended up stranded in a ditch. Everyone tried to find some solace from the biting dust by curling up inside the car and covering themselves with blankets. As the sand blasted the car, it sifted through the cracks and crevices of that old jalopy, filling their lungs with the dry, powder-like dust.

In contrast to the dust storms, Dad often told the story of the blizzard of 1949. That winter storm to beat all storms dumped more than four feet of snow on the countryside, and the relentless winds created drifts more than twenty-feet deep. After the storm ended, a tunnel had to be dug through an enormous snow drift in order to reach the outhouse so that personal needs could be met without using bedpans or cooking pots. I'm sure a lot of bouncing around and crossing legs was involved in the wait to finally reach the outside facility. The wind chill, combined with the weight of the heavy snow actually froze the livestock, including cows and horses, into solid blocks of ice as they stood huddled together in an effort to survive the unprecedented, arctic storm. I loved to listen to Dad tell the story of how he was able to drive his old '46 Willy's Jeep across the countryside after the storm. He drove over the tops of the fence lines due to the snow being so deep and packed so hard from the cold and intensity of the storm.

Tales told how the ranch was originally furnished with kerosene lamps that provided light, and the coal stove that provided warmth and the means to cook the meals. Initially, there was no running water in the house. The only available water for cooking, cleaning and bathing had to be carried to the house from a close-by natural spring, which explains the ritual of only bathing on Saturday nights. Furthermore, it was too much work to keep refilling the tub, so the one who took the first bath with the hottest and cleanest water was lucky. Woe to the child who was at the end of the line, who bathed in the murky water saturated with dirt and soap. Of course, according to Dad, since he was the "boy" of the family, he was usually the last to dive in.

After the house was finished, Grandpa devised a gravity-feed system that provided the family with the luxury of piped-in water. Truly, this was a luxury for the day. It was typical of the ingenuity that homesteaders had to develop in order to survive in those desolate areas, miles away from civilization. During the 1940s Grandpa decided it was time to get rid of the kerosene lamps, and so he invested in a wind-charge electrical plant that utilized 12-volt battery power for lighting. Of course, he had to install it all himself, and since he was the first in the area to invest in this new technology, he had to rely on his wits and common sense to make it function properly. It was actually about eight years later before the Rural Electric Association brought electricity to that part of the county and real electric power came to be commonplace in all the ranches in the area.

There was the flash flood that came roaring down the normally dry Dead Horse Creek, filling the small ravine to overflowing after a severe thunderstorm. The torrential waters were so swift and violent that they washed out part of the bridge between the ranch and the small town of Snyder, which was about nine miles away. Dad had been on a date with his high school sweetheart (who would actually become Mom) when the storm hit. Upon driving back to the ranch late that night after dropping his date off at the front door (and I'm sure not leaving until he got a much anticipated good-night kiss), he went speeding down the gravel road in his 1947 Studebaker at speeds only a teenager would dare drive. Up ahead, where the bridge used to be, all he saw in the dim headlights was foaming, swirling, and tumultuous waters as they eroded a path across the road. He slammed on the brakes, coming within a few short feet of plunging into the turbulent ravine waters. A near-accident that could have changed my own destiny. Dad walked more than five miles in the dark across those rain-drenched, prairie hills to get home that night. He walked into the ranch house, just in time to go back out to the barn to milk the cows, since it was well past four o'clock in the morning and the cows were bellowing from their bloated discomfort.

As kids we thrilled to the stories of rabbit drives on the prairie where ranchers and all of their families would gather together to walk through the sage and yucca-dotted hills. The human chain would stretch out across the plains, beating pots and pans in an effort to herd the long-eared jack rabbits and cottontail bunnies into enclosed pens where they would then be slaughtered as a means for controlling the exploding populations.

There were stories of the long, tedious sun-drenched days of farming dry-land wheat. Farming in those days was completely different than today. There was no fancy, new-fangled farm equipment that provided pampered comfort to those poor, overworked farm hands and no shade-covered cabs with air conditioning, DVD players, Global Positioning Systems, or cell phones. There was no such thing as eight- or ten-hour days, but rather, long days that started before dawn and ended well after sunset. To add to the length of the day was the fact that the wheat fields were about fifteen miles from the ranch, near a little prairie town named Stoneham. The fields were accessible only by traveling down a dusty, narrow, gravel road with its washboard, rutted surface. In fact, Grandpa's wheat field had once been a heavily wooded area, at least at a time not too long after the foundations of the earth had been laid. At the time they were farming it, the earth contained the remnants of a long-forgotten petrified forest, which constantly required the removal of some of the most beautiful chunks of petrified wood that you could imagine. As Dad would plow and disk the field, he would unearth some pretty hefty chunks of the ancient trees, then he would have to stop, pick them up and haul them away before the field could be planted. Some of those chunks were nearly four-feet long and twelve inches in diameter. He took those pieces back to the ranch where he built a long retaining wall running along one side of the drive that led into the combination garage, shed, and granary. That retaining wall was a constant reminder that this world contained a lot of ancient history. History that occurred well before our time, and history that would continue on long after we were gone.

One of the most unusual aspects of the ranch was the natural spring that fed into the pond, which was always referred to as "the fishin' hole." Grandpa had engineered and built the pond not too far from the ranch house. On a hot summer day, it served as a refreshing oasis for enjoying a cool retreat from the dry, baking heat of the prairie grasslands. When Dad was a boy he even rigged up a diving board to spring forth into the deepest part of that refreshing oasis. Grandpa had stocked it with fish so it also became the much loved fishin' hole that provided later generations with infinite hours of unadulterated angling pleasure.

A sandy beach reached out along the dike side of this man-made paradise, with marshy grasses and cattails encompassing the remainder of the water's edge. The watery inhabitants of this mystical place included native snapping turtles, pollywogs, and bullfrogs that led the resonating chorus of God's hidden creatures singing forth throughout the summer evenings and late into the star-filled nights. This particular spot of God's beautiful creation called the "eastern plains" holds many special memories that remain locked securely away in the deepest recesses of my heart and mind.

Grandma and Grandpa Cook often shared the story of how both of their grandfathers had fought in the Civil War in the Northern Army and each of them spent some time as Southern prisoners of war. Fortunately, they both survived their ordeal, returning home after war's end to continue on with their lives. Stories like these piqued my imagination, while providing fascinating tidbits of information on my ancestry, my birthright. Actually, my heritage reached to many corners of the globe; from my pure-blooded, 100 percent Danish maternal-grandmother to royalty in Scotland, which provided a multitude of childhood visions that included castles, knights, and maidens' in distress, and, of course, battles with the infamous Loch Ness monster. The family heritage was extremely diverse, including genetic links to American presidents Ulysses S. Grant and Martin Van Buren, as well as French-Canadian trappers. Bloodlines included Cajuns of Louisiana and links to homesteaders in Oklahoma, Iowa, and Colorado, where great-grandparents were actually born on the dusty trails of the wagon trains heading west.

Our heritage included sailors of the U.S. Navy, along with soldiers who served as captains and colonels in the U.S. Army. We had relatives who shed their blood, and a few who gave their all in foreign countries so that freedom would ring forth throughout the world. In Europe, the

Pacific, Korea, and Vietnam, the sacrifice of numerous relatives had forever changed the landscape of those war-torn countries. Because of that sacrifice, which was made on our behalf, our heritage became a source of personal pride.

Ancestral names took on a significant importance to us as we listened to the stories of our genetic links to the distant past. These links included names like Williams of Littledean from England. The Petersons descended from ancient Vikings. The Grant clan settled in Scotland, but migrated from France, changing their name from LeGrand. Blush hailed from the region of the Swiss Alps. Daigle, originally D'Aigle, meant "the Eagle" in French. Finally, we come to Cook, our great Grandfather. On H.E. Cook's death certificate his mother's maiden name was listed as "unknown," leading to speculation about where her ancestry originated. Haskell, Frees, Gilbert, Gilliland, Weber, and Davis—the list goes on to prove that our family is truly American. Within our veins flow the genetic links of many civilizations, cultures and nationalities, making our family a virtual melting pot of genetic lineage.

Our forefathers (and foremothers) came together during a brief moment in the history of the world, allowing us to be created in this particular moment of time for our own personal, individual, purpose. Who we are had been determined through the genetic links of previous generations, but who we were to become was dependent upon our own choices, along with the grace of God. This moment in time, which we had inherited from the distant past, had evolved into the time that Tim and I knew, and which we were blessed to share together.

While Dad and Tim's father, Uncle Don, served as examples of what it means to be a man and a father by their positive role modeling, Mom and Aunt Dorothy served more as our spiritual and emotional guides. That's not to say Dad and Don weren't committed to their faith. But rather, Tim and I in a lot of ways could have been considered, at least in a proverbial way, as "momma's boys." We were a bit pampered by our moms. After all, moms can pamper, and dads really aren't equipped to respond to kids in that way. Moms are there to kiss the hurts and mend the boo-boos. They provide assurance and security that things will be okay, even when we would screw up. They provided lots of praise, along with much needed pats on the back. After all, boys do need to have someone to help build their egos through the tumultuous times of childhood, especially the teenage years.

Mothers listen when you talk, and our moms also had an innate ability to gracefully discipline us when we wandered off the straight and narrow path. It was Mom who made us get up all of those Sunday mornings to take us to Sunday school and church, when we would have much rather preferred to stay in bed or go outside to play. However, I'm grateful for that constant limit that my mom placed on my life because those seemingly endless, oftentimes boring moments within the confines of our little community church provided the foundation for my spiritual awakening and commitment to a faith that has lasted a lifetime.

Mom and Dorothy always shared a special closeness from the time Mom and Dad had married, or so I've been told. Both of them would readily admit that their camaraderie and bond escalated in 1956 when they both became expectant mothers. With that common experience they developed a close relationship which proved to be the forerunner of the years to follow. From the time I can remember, Mom was as close to Aunt Dorothy as she was to her own brother or sister.

I made my arrival first, checking in during the fall at 10:15 p.m. on October 15. I weighed in at a whopping 8.5 pounds. Mom and Dad always said my love for baseball stemmed from my birth during the World Series. I guess maybe that's why my older brother, Randy, always referred to me as a "big, ball baby." But then again, maybe not! My cousin wasn't due into the world until after the first of the year, but apparently he decided that rather than having our birthdays in different years, he'd come as an early Christmas gift on December 14. I like to think that he was too anxious to start our life together as best of friends, so he entered into this life about a month early. I sometimes think that it may have been his competitive spirit that brought him into the world early, and he didn't want to be left too far behind.

It seemed that even then, Tim and I couldn't wait to get acquainted to start out on life's adventures together. His adult body and six-foot frame belies the fact that he entered this world at a mere 4 pounds. Tim's premature delivery by almost three months required him to spend the first months of his life in a hospital fighting to survive. As soon as he was born at the Brush hospital, he was rushed to Denver in an effort to try to save his fragile life. At the time, the doctors didn't give him much of a chance to survive, but somehow, through God's grace and divine appointment, he did. His survival was probably due to the vast amount of prayer being lifted up.

Being the fighter that he was, Tim wasn't one to give up easily and he proved this from the day he entered this world. He carried a scar on his chest where the doctors placed a needle to inflate his collapsed lung immediately following his birth. As we grew up, he took pride in showing off this scar anytime the occasion arose. To him, it was a badge of courage, sort of a medal of honor, for it signified his fight into life and his conquest of death. It seems as though his survival was predestined, giving us the opportunity to grow up together, sharing life's sorrows and pains, it's joys and jubilations, and its peaks and its valleys. To be bonded together, not as mere cousins, but as blood brothers. To become through the years of close companionship, "Buddies forever."

The sun does rise, the sun does set, the moon shines bright at night;
God saw the "day" that He had made, and knew that it was right . . .

Pre-dawn days, Creation days, days born of time and space;
Earth's great wonders came to be, Through God's abounding grace.

Days of birth, genetic days, rich heritage displayed;
God breathes sweet life into each soul, great men this way are made.

Trail-crossed days, Kismet days, days of destinies,
The lives of many people, determine family trees.

Days of yore, days long past, In retrospect we see,
That trails of many distant paths, created you and me.

Paths emerged from long ago; but who and what we are,
Depends on fate of days now gone, and what's written in each star.

Days in the lives of new-born babes, Will span the gulf of time,
Soul-searching days, goal reaching days, bring days of heights sublime.

Those days of long past heritage, breathe life into each soul,
Days of purpose to each life born, brings time to reach "the goal."

"The goal" in life, "The goal" in death, our days are numbered here;
"A time to live, a time to die," our God is always near!

—Clarice D. Cook

CHAPTER 3

Lead Us Not Into Temptation

Even though we spent many days together as babies, one of my earliest memories of my cousin Tim was when he lived in a little house in Thornton, Colorado with his Mom and Dad and three sisters. Billee Dee was a year older than us. Laureli was four years older, and Cheri Lea was twelve years older. One time when we went to visit, neither my older brother, Randy, nor I were allowed to go into the house because Tim had the chicken pox. Reluctantly, we stood outside and waited for Mom and Dad to return.

We didn't stay too long on that visit, but it is still one of my most vivid memories of Tim. Ironically, this earliest, vivid memory would be prophetic of feelings I would experience nearly thirty years later when I last saw Tim. However at that time we were just two, tow-headed boys, standing at the storm door looking at each other, not able to enjoy the adventures a warm summer's eve had to offer. I wanted so badly for Tim to get better so we could frolic in the lingering rays of the setting sun.

It seems we spent our entire childhood together. Although we could only see each other a few times each week, we had that special chemistry that allowed us to immediately turn each meeting into an exciting and daring adventure. I always considered us a modern-day Tom Sawyer and Huck Finn. I don't know which one of us was Huck, but we were always scheming of things that many times got us into trouble. Yet, more times than not, our schemes brought hours of unadulterated fun.

Back in the 1950s before the world went "green" all families daily burned their trash in cement incinerators located in the backyards of most family homes. One day, Uncle Don had dumped a bunch of old paint cans in the incinerator. Tim and I stumbled onto those half-full cans and, like any curious four-year-old, had to investigate the contents of every can. It seemed like such a waste to throw away those delightful, colored cans, while the ugly cement incinerator cried out for a much needed sprucing up. So there we sat, two little tow-headed kids, all cleaned up to go shopping, finger painting the incinerator with brightly colored enamel paint. This kind of paint never came off so it could weather many years of storms. Actually, most of the paint didn't end up on the incinerator, but on us, which had a lot to do with the fact that four-year-old boys were still a bit lacking in the manual dexterity department. Although, I remember thinking that we were doing a super job as we sat laughing and giggling in the warm spring sun, prideful of our work as we imagined the sheer delight our mothers would find in our Picasso-inspired masterpiece.

When Mom and Aunt Dorothy came into the backyard to get us for the day's shopping excursion, we quickly realized that they weren't as impressed with our fine art as we had imagined. In fact, as soon as they walked out the door into the backyard, their screams foretold our fateful plight. "Lanny Kim Cook!" "Timothy Eugene Trusty!" The decibel level of our mothers' voices was a true indicator of the fine predicament that was awaiting us. Mothers, or maybe I should say parents in general, never use your full, given name unless you've just committed one of the Seven Deadly Sins. It was obvious that we had just committed Deadly Sin Number One of childhood, "Never, ever get dirty when you're all cleaned up and ready to go somewhere."

Frequently, as a child, I just didn't feel the appreciation I thought I deserved for my efforts. This was one of those times. Why, we had worked our little chubby fingers to the bone to try to beautify an otherwise dismal piece of concrete architecture. All we got in return was a lot of mumbling as our mothers took turpentine to our extremities. For the next hour or so, all they could do was complain about the mess we had made of ourselves as they relentlessly scrubbed. Aunt

Dorothy muttered under her breath a few words of wisdom about Uncle Don and what was waiting for him when he got home. These were words of wisdom that little four-year-old ears knew their mouths should never repeat, unless of course, they wanted to rile their parents. Even at such a young age, I was sure glad that I wasn't around when Uncle Don got home from work. But, knowing him, he probably laughed it off with that big guffaw that was uniquely his. It seemed at the time that our mothers just didn't have a true appreciation for our artistic tendencies. Maybe we really weren't budding Picassos, but Tim and I agreed that they had the coolest looking incinerator of anyone on the block.

I don't remember whether we went shopping or not, after our close encounter with the enameled kind, but I do remember learning on one of those shopping trips that Deadly Sin Number Two of childhood can not only be painful on a youngster's backside, but it can also be a rather embarrassing moment for that little one's momma. Of course, that added embarrassment increased the pain level on a young *gluteus maximus*. I sometimes wonder how Tim and I ever survived a shopping excursion with our mothers. When they went shopping, time stood still. I really believe that they hold some sort of record for taking the most time deciding whether or not to buy one particular dress.

Anyone who has ever gone shopping with a woman knows exactly what I'm talking about. Tim and I endured this stroll through fashion city for what seemed like an eternity. I'm surprised we didn't have to start shaving before our mom's finished shopping that day. We were so bored that we could hardly contain ourselves. In fact, there is a law of physics which helps explain why we acted the way we did. It has to do with the law of energy. Any normal four-year old contains a vast amount of kinetic energy (which is energy in motion.) That much energy won't allow anyone, let alone a four-year old, to sit still for any substantial length of time. When anyone attempts to contain two full doses of kinetic energy into one shopping cart, there is a chemical reaction that produces a hormone that directly effects the better judgment gland. Of course, the reset button for this gland is located directly below the lower lumbar region of a young child's backside.

As this chemical imbalance affected our judgment, Tim and I crawled out of the shopping cart. Releasing our stored up energy, we chased each other through the racks of that year's latest fashion. Mom and Dorothy were too engrossed in shopping to notice our antics, which increased the rush of hormones to our better judgment gland. Since we were still operating under that old object-permanence phase of life (the psychological theory of, "If we can't see you, then you can't see us"), we upped the ante on our shenanigans. We both realized that this was the perfect opportunity to find out the answer to that age-old question that has plagued humanity for centuries: "What do mannequins look like underneath those dresses?" We had hardly gotten a peek under that dress when we felt the wrath of mom being generously applied to our better judgment gland's reset button. It wasn't just a slight swat by a slightly irritated mother either. It was the kind of swat that nightmares are made of and the kind that could leave a mark. Of course, this was back in the day when social services encouraged some real discipline for juvenile delinquents.

When we looked up we could tell by the glowing embers in our mothers' eyes that we had over-stepped the boundary of good taste, and good judgment. Mom picked me up so high and so fast that I thought I was going to be the first kid on the moon, and that was years before the Project Mercury space program was even in existence. It wasn't the liftoff either with all of the stress of negative "G's" (the measurement of gravitational force due to increased acceleration), that left a long-lasting impression on me, it was my re-entry and splash down. The rest of the trip Tim and I spent behind bars, confined to separate shopping carts in solitary confinement. I can still feel those cold metal bars pressing against my rosy little cheeks as I gazed out at the world from my state of penal isolation.

Childhood's Deadly Sin Number Three is, "Don't play with matches." Tim and his sister Billee had a mild case of warts when they were little and, of course, like all kids they wanted to rid themselves of those embarrassing blemishes. After all, from a child's perspective, old warts were associated with old witches. Who wants that stereotype following you around in school? One day Billee came up with what sounded like a great idea to remedy their plight. She had heard that warts were removed by burning them off. As a sophisticated seven-year-old, she found some matches and tried to convince Tim and me to attempt the delicate medical procedure. She used all her feminine persuasion to try and convince us that it would be painless, effective, and, most importantly, that our folks would never find out about any medical malpractice.

She had done a pretty fair job of convincing our wary little hearts, but we couldn't decide who would take charge of the procedure and who would be responsible to assist in the operation. I picked up a match and nervously lit it, but as I slowly moved it toward the wart, my shaky little hands caused the flame to go out. Since I seemed incapable of proceeding with this delicate procedure, Tim decided to take over the operation. (Tim was a devout fan of *Ben Casey*, a television show about a doctor's exploits.) He lit a match, as he slowly, cautiously moved toward his sister's hand, but alas, to Billee's dismay, Dr. Tim didn't have the nerve to perform under the extreme pressure either.

Just about that time, their sister, Laureli came out on the back porch. "What are you guys doing?" she shrieked. Still screaming, "You're not supposed to be playing with matches! I'm going to tell Mom!" she grabbed the box of matches and ran back into the house. A sibling that has caught you red-handed with the goods is like a cat who has caught the mouse and deviously terrorizes it for a while. They encircle you with their paws, swatting you around like a toy, sadistically enjoying the power of having your life in their control. Every time you think you see an escape route, they swat you back into the reality that your existence is in their control.

We knew that we were going to be dead meat after she ratted us out to our folks. But Laureli had this big sister thing down to a science. She never did let the cat out of the bag, or in this case, the rats out of her sight. That's not to say that we didn't have to pay the price for flirting with one of the Deadly Sins. No sir. She held it over our heads for months like a guillotine hanging by a thread. Our lives, well, at least the welfare of our *gluteus maximus's,* were hanging in the balance. So, in the process of learning about the ramifications of Deadly Sin Number Three of childhood, we learned a great lesson about Deadly Sin Number Four of childhood, "If you're going to do something wrong, never, ever do it in sight of a sibling. It will come back to bite you in the butt, one way or another."

There were several Deadly Sins of childhood that Tim and I didn't learn about together, but we did share experiences with each other in our attempts to save the other some undue pain, agony, and suffering. I found out about Deadly Sin Number Five of childhood one day in church when I was about five years old. Mom, Dad, Randy and I had gone down to Snyder one weekend in the early spring to visit with both sets of grandparents. Snyder wasn't much of a town anymore, but there were still a host of dated, deteriorating structures littered throughout the hamlet. They stood as a haunting reminder that at one time this was a hustling and bustling community.

Snyder was a ghost-capitol of the once vast, western cattle empire, and served as a central shipping point to the eastern markets after the steel rails of the Union Pacific Railroad were laid in 1881. The town was nestled among the tall, cottonwood trees on the South Platte River valley of Northeastern Colorado. The town had once sat at a crossroad where the Overland stage trail wound its way west along the river. The trail crossed the Arapahoe and Cheyenne trails and led to the cool, refreshing, life-saving waters of the gently flowing river. During its hey-day the town was a bustling, growing, economic agricultural center for the northeastern plains region. But for whatever reason, it had died out. All that was left were a few dozen homes, two small churches, a small convenience store, the local bar, the post office, a gas station, and a service garage. Even still, there were a multitude of aging, dilapidated remnants of a more prosperous time that had spurred the development and prosperity of this quaint, little town.

The old, two-story mercantile building sat next to the grocery store and locker plant that Grandma and Grandpa Williams had built and operated. Mom had worked in this family operation too, after school while growing up. But, due to hard economic times, the store closed down and stood abandoned. The aged mercantile building with its faded red paint was still standing in my early years, and it looked as if it had come straight out of the western movies depicting the early 1800s. The weathered wooden siding drooped toward the ground. Old nails that secured the pieces together grew weaker daily as rust ate at their once-strong carbon steel spines. The wooden sidewalk that extended the length of the building squeaked and cracked with the weight of anyone who dared trek across those aged planks of oak. The wooden awning that sheltered the wooden walkway below jutted out from under the second-level living quarters that sagged between six rotting posts that had seen decades of neglect.

An old, red, glass-topped gas pump had been added years later in front of the store; it stood as an ominous reminder of a bygone era, dating back to the Great War of the early 1900s. The old rail "hitching post," where the visiting cowhand's horses or the more prominent citizen's horse and buggies were tied, endured for many a year beside that old gas pump. These relics were a visual testimony of the merger between the "Wild West" and man's progress in the modern "Industrial Age." The hitching post was no longer a necessity in the life of the dying cow town, and neither was the old gravity-fed gas pump. This confluence of two different eras had been transformed to serve as a gathering place for the youth of the town who would congregate and sit on the weather-worn posts while they munched on after-school snacks of peanuts and Pepsi. Here in this rustic location, teen-agers of the community discussed the issues of their day, spread school gossip, and of course put on some airs, while practicing the fine art of flirtation in order to impress the members of the opposite sex. It was the teen-age town hangout, the meeting place. It was here at the old hitching rail that romance sprouted, as well as, the place where many a teen-age heart was broken.

At one time, Snyder had both an elementary school and a high school. The spirits of classes past could almost be felt as you peered through the dust-covered windows into the empty rooms of the abandoned buildings. As cousins, we loved wandering around the old school buildings, peering through the windows to try and catch a glimpse of the life our parents knew as children. The antiquated livery building personified the old western architecture of much of the town. It too stood empty with its windows and doors boarded up as it stood ominously across the street from the old mercantile store. The faded barn-red paint and padlocked double-wide doors indicated that it too had long since been abandoned and neglected, allowing Colorado's harsh seasons to take a toll on its massive wooden architecture.

Walking through Snyder was like walking through an old ghost town, everywhere you looked you could see abandoned remnants of a nearly forgotten era. The blacksmith shop that continued serving the farming community for years after most "Smithy's" had long since abandoned their trade was converted into an auto mechanic's garage. At one time an old creamery, where farmers brought cream, milk, butter and eggs to sell every Saturday morning, stood in the middle of the road. Restaurants and two barber shops once abuzz with business laid long-since forgotten. The little town even boasted a fine brick building that was built to house the bank. It came complete with an enclosed eight-foot square secured vault. In later years, Grandpa Williams and his brother Elwood converted the bank into a grocery store and post office. It was in this store that Mom first worked at the age of twelve even though by that time the store had changed ownership and it was no longer a family business. Down by the railroad tracks just a few hundred yards from the river, was a lumber yard and a train depot, which was equipped with the towns own telegraph.

The aging town was a pastoral scene straight out of a Norman Rockwell painting. Remnants of thriving businesses lay scattered among the old houses, home to the mostly aging inhabitants of this dying community. Many of those houses served as businesses before they were renovated and remodeled into homes. Grandma and Grandpa Williams's house was the old Russell Hotel, before the second floor was transformed into two large bedrooms and the flat roof replaced with a pitched roof, complete with dormers. The Russell Hotel was one of three hotels that served the needs of the once-booming cow town. Grandma and Grandpa had bought the house and Grandpa remodeled it in the late 1930s. The hand-powered water pump stood beside the house, contained within a dilapidated, white picket fence, which was always referred to as the "pump house."

It was obvious, even in the days of my youth, that the town had deteriorated from its glory days. One of the few things it had left to offer its inhabitants was a distinct connection to the past. The two churches, however, were still an active part of life in the small town and surrounding farm community. People would gather together on Sunday mornings to listen to an itinerant, seminary-student preacher who would drive in from Denver to share a message. One of my fondest memories is walking with my folks and my grandparents on those brisk Sunday mornings when we would spend the weekends in Snyder. Something almost magical about that walk was reminiscent of a Thomas Kincaid painting. We would trek down the long, narrow, cement sidewalk at Grandma's house through the property's gardens and grass lawns. We would open up the old, rickety-gate of the white picket fence to head up a dirt-covered alley toward the church. Three generations of family, walking hand-in-hand, brought an amazing amount of security into my life as a child.

The Methodist Church in Snyder held a special place in the hearts of all our family. Mom was raised in that small, stucco church as Grandma served as the Sunday school superintendent and Grandpa served as a caretaker for the building and grounds in his spare time. The church had added significance to us, because Grandma would often tell how her father had helped build the original, white clapboard church complete with a belfry and a bell with a welcoming chime that rang out every Sunday morning. That original church was destroyed in a fire in the early 1940s and was replaced by the new stucco place of worship that we came to know and love. Unfortunately, the bell was also destroyed in the fire when it fell from its lofty belfry. Silencing the cherished sounds that echoed across the river valley as the beginning of services were announced to the township each week. My older brother Randy, along with my younger brother, Danny, and I were all baptized in the church as babies. It was a tradition that had started generations earlier as Mom, Grandma and Grandpa Williams had all taken the step of faith in that small country church. Every weekend that we spent with our grandparents in Snyder, we faithfully attended Sunday services in that quaint little place of worship. The lessons, along with the reverence that I feel whenever I attend a church service, are directly tied to those precious days of worship that I experienced with my loving grandparents and parents in Snyder.

My earliest memories of the church in Snyder spring from one Sunday during communion service. Every congregation that participates in the commemoration of the Lord's Supper serves the elements in a variety of ways. Some churches use juice, others use wine; some use wafers, while others use bread. Sometimes communion is served in the pews, while other times it is served individually by the pastor at the front of the sanctuary. On this particular Sunday, as was the custom in the Snyder Methodist Church, communion was served in the front at the communion rail. Since I was too young to understand communion complexities, Mom and Dad, along with my grandparents, left Randy and I unattended in the pews, with the admonition of "Sit still and be quiet!"

This was probably the first time I had ever been left "unattended" during a worship service. All of the adults were at the front of the church, kneeling at the rail, getting a little snack to eat and a little something to drink. All I could do was sit there looking cute and trying to behave myself. "Cute?" I knew I was cute. People were always telling Mom how cute I was. I had the gift of being "cute." In my young little mind, I knew that this was the perfect opportunity to take advantage of my gift of "cute!" Nobody could see me, since they were all up front, with their heads bowed and their eyes closed. Everyone *except* that gorgeous little four-year old blonde babe that was sitting in the pew right behind me. For as long as I can remember, I have had a thing for "cute, younger women."

"What can I do to impress this cute young babe?" I thought for a moment. And then it came to me, "What is the cutest thing in the world to a younger woman?" The little voice in my head quickly replied, "Why, it's a puppy dog!"

So, I quickly crawled down off of the pew, got onto all fours, and started panting, with my tongue hanging out in my finest puppy imitation. It was obvious that I wasn't making any headway in impressing this young lass, and I could see that she was pretty capable of ignoring my advances. Either that, or she was just plain stuck up. But I couldn't let it end like this, as I stood there on all fours, I knew I had to do something a little more daring in order to get her attention. Yes, right there and then, I decided it was time to take it to the next level and crank it up a notch. I crawled underneath the pew, and peeked up at her, trying to draw her in with my cute-as-could-be puppy dog eyes. "Nothing!" Boy was she ever playing hard to get! In total desperation, and clearly without thinking it through, I began to bark. Not just a timid, little "ruff, ruff!" But rather, a loud, defending the home-front bark! Not just once, but "Bow-wow-wow-wow-wow-wow. Ouch!" I yelped, as my feet left the ground and I found myself flying in mid-air. I thought I was being lifted up by the hands of God. In fact, I would have preferred to see the loving face of my Maker when I came to my senses after being lifted up about eight feet off the ground, spun around in mid-flight and coming face to face with my molester. Well, actually, it wasn't a molester, but also wasn't who I thought it would be either. It wasn't Mom, it was Dad. I could bat my cute little puppy dog eyes at Mom, whimper a little bit, and I could probably get off with a suspended sentence. But no, this was Dad and boy was he mad, or maybe I should say embarrassed! "Mommm . . . , Graandma . . . , Graandpa . . . , Saaave me . . . !" I shrieked out.

I had never seen Dad so mad in all of my life. He swept me out the doors of that church so fast that I think I received third-degree wind burns. Dad had never spanked me before, at least not that I could remember. He had always left corporal punishment up to Mom. But this time I had made a major mistake in judgment! I was in for the biggest lesson of my short-lived life and for a moment, I thought I might be at the end of it. Dad didn't give one slight swat on the backside, he gave me more than I care to remember. I found out the hard way that you don't want to get spanked by somebody from the working class of society. His hands were way too strong and calloused from all the years of working the lumberyard to be applied to my tender, little *gluteus maximus*. But, boy was it ever effective.

Dad didn't take me back into the church after my lesson in doggie etiquette. Instead, he took me by the arm, pulling me back to Grandma's house down the elm-lined alley, dragging my feet along reluctantly in the sandy, country dirt. My resistance was accentuated by my horror-filled visions of what might still lie ahead. Especially since Dad had cut a good-sized "switch" off of one of those huge elm trees that lined the alley. I can still remember Dad telling me after the spanking to "straighten up and quit that crying!" Of course, one of his favorite lines as I was growing up, and one that I used on my own sons too was, "Now if you don't stop crying, I'll really give you something to cry about!" Although I could never say it, I always thought, "Gee Dad, what do you think just happened?"

However, when Dad would tell me that, I knew it was time to shut down the tear spigot, squelch the sobs, and straighten up! Fortunately for me, by the time we got back to Grandma's house, Dad realized that I had learned my lesson. The visions of terror that had infiltrated my tiny little head never transpired into reality as he tossed the elm switch by the wayside in the alley. I still thank God for having a father who was extremely slow to anger, and who knew when the punishment had taught a lesson that served its purpose.

From that point on, I had a great respect for the reverence of God's holy sanctuary. I learned that Deadly Sin Number Five of childhood is probably one of the most important lessons to learn as a youngster. "Never bring shame or embarrassment to your parents, especially in front of God and country!" Although, I still think that God must have found a bit of enjoyment in the antics of an innocent five-year old as he learned a lesson of reverence from his Father Almighty. I shared this lesson with Tim later on in life, after he started attending church with our family. I figured it was the least I could do, to save him from the wrath of an embarrassed parent. Tim and I learned many lessons in life that dealt with the Deadly Sins, some by ourselves and others together. Part of the joy of growing up with a very close, special friend is being able to share the important lessons in life. Some of those lessons came early on in life, while many others came as we grew older. It was later on in life that we actually learned a lesson about the last of the Deadly Sins.

Yes, those childhood days marked times of adventure when we would play for hours in make-believe worlds of pirates, cowboys and Indians, cops and robbers. Tim used to have an old rocking horse that Uncle Don had rigged up on his swing set. One night when Tim and I were playing cowboys and Indians, I hopped on that horse to make my getaway as Tim was just inches away from taking my scalp. Well, when I jumped onto that plastic steed, that old horse bucked me off so fast that I didn't know what had hit me. I landed flat on my back which knocked the wind out of me, leaving me gasping for air as stars twinkled around my head like I was a cartoon character.

Uncle Don had just walked out of the house and into the backyard as that horse had done me in. I couldn't see him amid echoes of the "last roundup," but I could hear him laughing all the way back into the house. Of course, Tim ended up victorious as he took his make-believe knife to lift my scalp, but that wasn't the worst of it. I couldn't bring myself to go back into the house to face the folks after this little buckaroo had been bucked off that makeshift old nag of a horse. So, Tim and I decided to lay low, sneaking off into his bedroom in an effort to maintain a low profile and to save face. In this particular instant, it was my reddened face and bruised posterior. That was an example of the camaraderie that we shared. We could tease each other, but we would never let anyone else pick on the other, that is if either of us could help it.

Aunt Dorothy and Uncle Don moved around a lot back in our younger years and for a while it seemed that they were always moving into another home. They lived in Thornton for a time, before moving down to the small town of Brush where Don worked on the local police force and Dorothy went to the community college to become a nurse. They then moved to Littleton and finally back to Thornton. With every move, Tim and I would come up with new adventures as we explored the secrets of new neighborhoods, new houses, and discarded cardboard boxes. The move to Brush when Tim was in the second grade proved to be the beginning of his problems with school. Unfortunately, back in those days, schools really didn't assess student's abilities and provide programs to meet the learning needs or styles of the child. Tim's teacher never took the time or displayed an interest in helping with his slower reading ability. When school ended that year, he was held back in the same grade, which he repeated the next year.

From that time on, Tim had a bit of difficulty reading. He never was able to catch up in this subject, which of course impacted his studies in all subjects as he progressed through school. It wasn't that Tim wasn't smart enough, he was able to do anything he set his mind to as long as it didn't require him to do any extended reading. Reading was obviously laborious for him, slowing him down when he had something that needed to be done or something that he'd rather be doing. It always bothered me that he ended up a grade behind me and I resented his teacher for not doing more to help him. Although, I'm pretty sure it bothered Tim a whole lot more. However, we never let it interfere with our relationship or with our fun. As far as either one of us was concerned it really didn't make that much difference. If someone would mention it, we would act like we didn't hear anything and go about our business. I knew that schooling wasn't as easy for Tim as it was for me, so we would just avoid the subject. Neither one of us would intentionally say anything that would make the other feel inadequate, so when anybody would bring up how we were doing in school we would give them a pat answer of "just fine."

Our adventures together never involved any sort of book learnin' or school-type activities. Instead, we always found something to do that included running, chasing, exploring, building or creating, and we always had an amazing time enjoying our adventures together.

As I think back, I realize that one of the reasons our friendship was so special was because we were always turning our realities into an adventure that was created out of our own wild imaginations. Grandma and Grandpa Cook lived on the ranch that they homesteaded until we were about twelve years old. Many of our adventures took place out there in that dry, parched prairie and there are still significant aspects of the ranch that are forever etched in my mind.

During those days, our family would travel down to Snyder nearly every other weekend to visit both sets of grandparents. Snyder was about 90 miles away from Denver and the trip usually began on a Friday evening, culminating in a late drive back home on Sunday evening. On these weekends, we would always stay at mom's folks' house, but would usually go out on Saturday afternoons to visit dad's folks for a spell. It usually never failed that Tim would be there too with his family. The adults would go into the cobblestone house for a visit, while shooing the kids off to find some fun on their own. Many times we would head off to the big cottonwood trees that made up the windbreak behind the old ranch house. The house that Grandma and Grandpa Cook had painstakingly built out of cinderblocks and river rock.

In this make-believe Sherwood Forest, our imaginations would run wild with adventures of Robin Hood and his merry men. Those huge cottonwood trees would also provide the backdrop for our own haunted forest. Images of ghosts and goblins came to life as twisted, contorted branches cast an eerie shadow on the damp, mossy, mulch-covered ground below.

On other visits, we would head up to the pond for a bit of childhood angling, or to skip rocks off the crystal-clear waters. Each of those trips always included looking for arrowheads and Indian artifacts. I loved those trips up to the fishin' hole, because most of the time, Dad would only take a few of us there at a time. Many times it was just me and my brother Randy. Sometimes it would be me and Tim. Dad, who loved to fish, always led the way up the trail, well-armed with a fresh supply of worms dug up from the moist, damp earth on the north side of the ranch house. As the years went by our fishing group continued to grow to nearly a half-dozen young line-tanglers who all needed help in getting a worm on the hook and the line in the water. By this time with most of the cousins tagging along, Dad never got a whole lot of fishing done himself, since he was too busy untangling lines and baiting hooks.

One day, Grandpa Cook and his brother Charlie took pity on Dad, deciding to come along to give him a hand with this whole gaggle of pint-sized fish mongers. All three of them spent the first hour getting everyone else's lines in the water with the bobbers attached. They had just started talking about getting their own fishing tackle out to try their luck at the waters when Tim hooked and began reeling in a keeper. Tim reeled in a respectable old catfish, dragging him out of the water and clear up onto the shore. Uncle Charlie went over to help get the "cat" off the hook and in the creel. He kneeled down next to the flopping catch-of-the-day then cautiously latched onto it so as not to get stung by the spiny fins. He had just twisted the hook out of the fish's mouth when my cousin Rick went tearing along the water's edge, kicking the unattended fishing rod that was lying on the shore. The hook that Uncle Charlie had just removed from the fish's mouth suddenly and painfully found itself hooked around his index finger. Dad and Grandpa worked on that hook for quite some time to remove it, but to no avail. They ended up having to take him home to clip off the end of the hook with a pair of wire cutters before they were able to snake it out from around the bone. Needless to say, it brought a rather abrupt end to our day of angling at the old pond. Dad never did take the whole gang fishing again after that trip. He set a limit of four, requiring the catch to be at least 42 inches in order to be a keeper.

Oftentimes, Grandma would quickly tire of all of us being under foot, so she would send us out to the musty old chicken coop with its faded, red paint to collect the eggs. She always warned us not to pester the roosters and to keep an eye out for snakes as we entered the rickety, old barn-style door. Sometimes we would just trek down the half-mile gravel drive that connected the ranch to the main county road. Whenever we would take that walk, it would be all the cousins together. Our folks always directed the older kids to "keep an eye out" for the little ones. In fact, I can say this now, but the older cousins always made it a lot more exciting as they talked about snakes, coyotes, eagles or bobcats that would chase us down to carry us away if we weren't good. As we shuffled along the gravel drive with our youthful exuberance, we would laugh and giggle as we threw rocks and talked about how brave we would be if we came across a rattlesnake or any of those other critters. The one time that a snake did cross our paths, we all tore out of there like a rocket to Mars, yep, even the bigger kids.

Snakes, especially rattlesnakes, still cause my heart to leap out of my chest. But as a child, the sound of a rattler was the most terrifying noise I had ever heard. Our parents' dire warning, "Watch out for snakes," echoed in my mind that day when the coiled-up predator let out its spine-tingling rattle. Total fear overwhelmed us as we ran as fast as our legs could carry us back to the safety and security of the ranch house. It was at a very early age that I gained a great respect for those slithering, poisonous creatures—a respect that has continued on throughout my entire life. We all learned that the best way to deal with any snake is to put as much distance between you and the snake as possible, in the least amount of time. As an adult, I have learned to apply this principle to other threatening dangers, like politicians and government officials.

On the ranch, adventures seemed endless. There was always something to do, something to see, or something to discover. It's amazing how life on a ranch engages the imagination while arousing the curiosity of inquisitive young minds—the robin eggs resting in their nest, just within reach of a four-year-old who was perched on his daddy's shoulder—the big old hoot owl flying out of its nest, disturbed by the summer breeze as it rustled through the giant, green leaves of the cottonwood trees—the humungous, green bullfrog jumping off the lily pads into the crystal clear waters of the pond, just beyond the cattails—baby ducks waddling in formation behind their mother as they make their way back into the safety of the pond—a beautiful, ring-necked, rooster pheasant, strutting through the dew-covered grasses in the meadow. In a child's eyes there was so much to see, so much to learn. We knew that around every corner, around every clump of sagebrush or yucca plant, lurked a new adventure bringing renewed excitement to the heart of a child.

Some of the adventures out on the ranch brought unending pleasure, but there were a few that brought some unwelcome pain. Grandpa Cook's brother Charlie lived on his own homestead, down the road about a mile from the ranch. One day, Charlie decided that he was going to let us ride his old nag of a horse. She was slightly sway backed, graying around the eyes and snout. It was obvious that she had seen her better days, even though she wasn't quite ready to make an appearance at the glue factory. Charlie saddled her up before leading her out to the graveled county road that ran parallel to his ranch. Our excitement grew as Randy, Tim, Billee and I jockeyed, (no pun intended, well, okay, maybe it was) for positional riding order. Charlie decided that one of the bigger kids needed to ride along with each of us little ones. This of course, meant that since Randy was the only bigger kid around, he would get to ride the entire time. After giving Randy a two-minute, Reader's-Digest version of horse-riding etiquette, Charlie helped him get his foot in the stirrup and boosted him onto the horse.

I was filled with unbridled anticipation as Charlie lifted me up on the horse, sitting me on the back half of the saddle right behind my brother. The smell of ranch life permeated the air, the smells of the ragweed and sage that covered the rolling hills filled our nostrils, along with the stringent aroma of old farm equipment. We sat there on old Nellie, like a couple of experienced cowhands, breathing in the smells and taking in the sights that can only be appreciated by one who is mounted on the back of a noble steed. Then, as the old girl raised her tail, the true stench of what ranches are known for engulfed us with the smell of fresh horse patties. Tim and Billee were bouncing in anticipation of their turn as they stood on the other side of the barrow pit in knee-high tumbleweeds. They were so excited they could hardly stand still, squirming, giggling, and picking on each other with childlike anticipation. Charlie's last words to Randy before he let loose of the reins was actually more of a command.

"Before you get to the top of the hill to turn around, dismount so you can lead her back home. Once she turns around and sees the barn, she'll be off like greased lightning to head back to her stall."

I'll be the first to admit that my older brother always had the hearing of an eighty-year-old. However, as we've both grown older, I now realize it was more of a case of "convenient, hearing dysfunction." I really think that he was just bullheaded enough to really believe he was "man" enough at eleven years old to ride galloping, greased lightning. Well, when we got to the top of the hill, old Nellie slowly turned herself around and I knew that we were in big trouble. My heart started to beat so hard and so loud, I couldn't even hear myself scream out, "Uncle Charlie told you to. . ."

The most exciting 200 yards of my short-lived life was probably when Nellie took off like greased lightning. Actually, it was more like WD-40, silicone-enhanced lightning. Unfortunately, we were about a half a mile from the ranch house as my fears quickly turned into reality with a thunderous, painful plop. I still say that it wasn't falling off old Nellie that hurt so bad, it was the sudden stop at the bottom of the ditch that really caught my attention. I remember Charlie picking me up out of the tumbleweed-covered barrow pit from alongside the road. He was laughing so hard I thought he was going to burst. This short, little rotund version of a man was gasping for his breath almost as hard as I was. Between his bursts of laughter, he'd pick out the sagebrush stuck in my hair and on my clothes. As he dusted the dirt and grass off of my britches, he'd regain his composure, before letting out another snort, followed by another burst of unadulterated laughter. My only consolation was that I ended up about twenty-five yards further down the road than my big cowboy of a brother.

By the time we walked back to the ranch, good ole Nellie was already in the barn, standing in her stall, her reins hanging to the ground while she serenely munched on a mouthful of hay. It seemed to me that she had a smirk of contentment on her face as she reared her head back, showed us her teeth, and let out a boastful neigh. She was seemingly pleased with herself for a job well-done, and rejoicing in the havoc she had just rendered in the lives and backsides of a couple of young tenderfoots. I'm sorry to say that our ride brought an abrupt end to the trail riding experience and Tim and Billee never got their turn. I've often wondered if they ever did forgive us for ruining their chance to ride that old, gray nag, or if deep down in their hearts they were thanking their lucky stars that Randy and I rode that blessed beast first.

Yes, in a child's eyes there was so much to see and to do. I remember Tim and I sitting on Grandpa's old tractor with the big steel wheels which sat abandoned beside the faded, red barn. We would sit side by side in that rusted, metal seat plowing the fields of our tender little minds for hours at a time. I can still smell that old, greasy tractor and I can still feel the heat of the sun-faded metal reflecting the afternoon heat waves into our faces, while we sat there jostling with the steering wheel and stretching our short little legs to push down on the clutch pedal. It always seemed like the end of the world when Dad would yell out in his tenor voice, for the third or fourth time, "C'mon, it's time to *go*!" And we'd have to bring our adventures to a temporary close. Temporary that is, until the next time we were together.

It's funny, in my memory I don't see Tim sitting there beside me on that old tractor, or shuffling along the gravel road, but I do feel his presence and his companionship. Our childhood was spent nurturing a friendship as our paths took us down the trail toward adulthood. What we were, as well as what we were to become was molded by those carefree days in the sun. Our friendship became the catalyst that surpassed the bonds of being mere cousins. When I think back fondly on those long-ago times, Tim was always there. It seems as though we were always together. Where he went, so would I. When we were together we were inseparable. We were more than just buddies, we were bonded together. We grew up being buddies forever, not just 'til life ends.

The sun does rise, the sun does set, the moon shines bright at night;
    God saw the "day" that He had made, and knew that it was right . . .
Childhood days, carefree days, Days filled full of joy,
    Days enmeshed by time and space, in the lives of two small boys.
Summer days, winter days, spring and autumn, too;
    Each and every day o'er flowed, with all the things to do!
From baby days to manhood, the days were filled with fun;
    No day was ever wasted, No day was really done.
Laughter, shouts and giggles, Echoed through the air;
    Conspirators in action, the world was theirs to share.
From rattles, balls and baby things, to trikes and bikes and skis,
    Fishin' poles and golfin' gear—they had a need of these.
Days of playful pretense, when stories come alive,
    Cowboys, Indians, Pirate games, how did these boys survive?
"Robin Hood" and "Big John" too, spent hours in the woods,
    Along with all the "Merry Men," they shared their borrowed goods.
Days of unknown artistry, when "Van Goghs" shine and bloom;
    Fame can soon become short-lived, with a mother's voice of doom!
"Up de lazy riber" days, Emprise as "Tom" and "Huck,"
    "We'll get this raft a floatin', with just a little luck."
These were the famous "whitewash kids," In days of long ago,
    Were they dressed in Sunday best, did their painting bring them woe?
Learning days, growing days, Time comes to go to school,
    The "lesson" learned in early life, Is to "Follow every Rule . . ."

—Clarice D. Cook

CHAPTER 4

"Summer's Magic"

There is nothing more magical or mystical than an early morning sun warming the moist, night-cooled beaches along a Colorado lakeshore as dawning rays of radiant light glisten off smooth crystal water. The morning sun was almost blinding as I lethargically crawled to the tent's open door, peeking out to see what the new day had to offer. There was never any sleeping in during those days at the lake. After all, it seemed like there was never enough time to take advantage of all the things to do and the fun to be had. It never mattered which kid would wake up first, we would always rouse the others out of bed. It also didn't make any difference how early any youngsters would get up, the folks would already be up and motivating. Life at the lake was almost like life on the farm where the entire family was up and moving well before the crack of dawn.

As soon as we were out of the tent with our swimming suits back on, it was off to the shoreline to check on the boats or to start a fire in the makeshift pit in order to take the nip off the cool morning air. Sometimes we would go straight down to the lakeshore with our fishing tackle in hand, ready to throw a line into the crystal clear water. The water in the mornings was so calm and transparent that the seemingly wash-boarded sands of the lake bottom would glow with glistening black, gold and silvery hues. The rich earth would reflect rays of sunlight back up through the tranquil water. We always paid a visit to all of the campers in our sometimes massive group of weekend water-skiing warriors to bid them all a hearty "good-morning!" There was one thing that could be said about Tim, Billee, Danny, and I, when it came to the people we knew, we were all extremely friendly.

We began our skiing weekends when Tim and I were about eleven years old. The excursions began when our families were invited by Lea and Al who were related to Aunt Dorothy through her first marriage. Al had a boat, along with a pickup and camper that they used nearly every weekend at one of the many lakes around Colorado's Front Range. The couple comprised two of the most gracious and fun-loving folks I had ever known. They were truly the outdoor types who loved to hunt, fish, boat and ski. The endless pleasure that we experienced on those trips was due to Lea and Al's gracious hospitality. Actually, a lifetime of enjoying the sports of boating and waterskiing can all be attributed to their initial invitation to tag along on their weekend excursions. The couple soon became great friends, causing all of us youngsters to affectionately refer to them as "aunt" and "uncle" even though there was no blood relation between any of us.

The fresh smell of country air was enhanced by the mouth-watering aroma of coffee brewing in campers, along with the smell of simmering bacon, flapjacks bubbling on the hot griddle and the smell of sweet melons being cut into pieces for breakfast. We would hover around the campers with stomachs growling and taste buds salivating, waiting anxiously for the world's three most long-awaited words, "Time to eat!" Every meal at the lake was like a feast. Mom and Dorothy always prepared enough food to feed a marching army. Maybe that was because with this group of camping fools gathered at the lake, there were more than enough hungry mouths to feed and there was never much of anything left over to feed the birds. Sometimes there were six or seven families with their campers, tents, boats, along with kids galore accompanied by a fine repertoire of family pets. There were so many people who came along that were friends of friends, and shirt-tail relations, that we often didn't know who was in our camping entourage. We most certainly never knew all of their names. Once Dad was in the boat riding along with Al. As he pulled a skier with his sixteen-foot boat, Al turned around to see who was skiing. He asked Dad, "Who the heck is this kid?" Dad turned around to take a look and after a few seconds responded, "I have no clue, I thought you knew who he was!" Regardless of who brought who to the lake, everyone was accepted and made to feel welcome. I'm sure that anyone already camped at the lake hated to see our entourage pulling in to the lake's campground as it always looked like an invading army, although our group was never obnoxiously loud or overbearing. There was never any loud music, drinking of alcohol, or being annoying or offensive, we were just a rather large, fun-loving group who took up a whole lot of campsites.

Lea and Al patiently taught all of us to ski as they shared their love of the sport with whoever was willing to join the fun. I didn't try skiing until the second summer after Mom, Dad and Randy had all mastered the sport. Mom had this paranoia about her eleven-year-old drowning or getting eaten alive by some sea monster lurking underneath the waves of that prairie oasis. It wasn't until she had experienced both the pains and pleasures of skiing that she agreed to allow me to try it for myself. It was rather funny though, watching her try to master those wooden slats. She spent the first summer hanging on to the rope as the boat dragged her around the lake with her backside bouncing off the water like a rock skipping across a pond. She was black-and-blue all over before she finally figured out the concept that you're supposed to stand up on the skis, instead of leaning backward while hanging on for dear life. She still swears that she drank half of the lake before she finally learned how to do it right. Actually, it wasn't until Dad finally drove the boat for her in a gentle, slower fashion that she stood up like you're supposed to, and continued skiing completely around the lake without falling. After that, she was hooked and even got to the point that she could ski with Al's "full throttle—full speed ahead—all the time" attitude, on only one ski, no less!

Dad and Randy both quickly learned to master the sport. In fact, they both looked as if they had been skiing for years the first time they ever tried. So, after a year of whining, begging and groveling, Mom finally gave into my pleas, my puppy dog eyes, and my pouty lower lip, which I might add, after years of perfecting, was one of the best in the world. Finally, she let me try skiing. I'm so thankful that she had finally learned how to enjoy the sport for herself, otherwise I would have probably had to run off as a teenager to join a water-skiing circus in order to try it out for myself.

The first time I attempted to ski, my heart raced with anticipation, while the cool water of the fresh-water lake added to the exhilaration of finally getting a chance to skim across the water like a graceful dolphin. Mom, Randy and Aunt Lea stood around me in chest-deep water helping to steady my balance, while pulling the skis up underneath me. Randy helped hold the rope tight so that there wasn't any slack in it, while all three simultaneously offered well-intentioned advice and instructions that I couldn't decipher or even begin to comprehend. Of course, I would have never remembered any of their words of wisdom as soon as Al hit the throttle to violently jerk me out of the water. Besides the constant chatter of the three of them talking over each other, the worst part of the ordeal was trying to stay upright in that bulky, awkward Mae West life jacket that I was forced to wear. Not only did the jacket constantly roll you over to face head down in the water, but it tipped my head back so far I couldn't see so I thought I would drown too!

Finally, after what seemed like hours of preparation, which of course was only minutes, I was finally ready. I was not only sitting stable in the water with the skis tucked neatly beneath me, but I had worked up the courage to finally give it a shot. I shouted out the proverbial, "Hit it!" and Al gave it full throttle. The old Mercury engine let out a mighty roar, while the blue exhaust bellowed out in a cloud of noxious gases. The boat leapt forward through the water, curling the water away from its stern like chips off a wood plane. I held tight to the slippery handle of the rope with unyielding determination as I anticipated my arms being jerked out of their sockets by the outboard engine's immense power. In the twinkling of an eye, I was standing on my own, as if I were walking on water, like Peter in the Bible, who stepped out of the boat and walked toward Jesus. I was skiing, it was almost like I was flying. Then, suddenly, I was falling flat on my back, squirming like a fish out of the water, making a magnificent splash before sinking below the surface into the watery depths of that lake. Flailing like a gooney bird on takeoff, relentlessly thrashing in a near state of panic, I desperately tried to get my head above water. It seemed like an eternity, although it was only a few seconds. Finally, I reached the surface, gasping for oxygen, spitting out water, while trying to wipe wet hair out of my eyes. With all of the instruction my coaches had given me before I started the trip, I had forgotten the most important advice of all, "Keep your mouth shut, dummy, when you fall!" Of course, that advice came from my loving older brother. Coughing and gasping, my nose stung from the intrusion of water into passages of my body where water was never intended to flow.

Dad was riding in the boat, ready to save me just in case I needed saving. "Are you okay?" he nervously inquired as the boat circled around me. "Yeah!" I exclaimed as I coughed, snorted, and sputtered in an attempt to clear the water out of my sinuses and airways.

"Do you want in?" Dad asked. "Nope, I'm going to try it again!" I quickly replied with unwavering determination.

I struggled to get the skis back in the proper position below me as I latched onto the floating ski rope encircling me. Struggling a bit to tread water, hold the rope, and to keep from letting that cumbersome lifejacket roll me over, I began to focus on the challenge at hand. Al eased the boat forward to pull the slack out of the rope, I leaned back while allowing the rope to begin to gently pull me forward toward the deep waters of the lake. I quickly elevated my position, adjusted the skis with the tips protruding out of the water, wrapped my arms around my knees in an effort to keep the skis from floating to the surface, tried to remember all of the instructions, including "Keep your mouth shut, dummy." Then, I quickly said a prayer. I closed my eyes before taking one last deep breath and yelling out again, "Hit it!"

I had prepared myself for the worst by pondering how long I'd have to hold my breath this time, because I feared how deep I would sink again if I fell. But, as the boat pulled me out of the water, I found that I was on top of those crystal, smooth waters, skimming across the surface like a kite on a string. I couldn't believe it, and it was such a relief to be able to stand up, and to keep standing up. After skiing along for at least a few hundred yards, I realized with a gasp, that I could quit holding my breath. "Hey dummy," I heard my brother's voice in my head, "You can breathe now!" What an amazing experience that was to inhale the sweet smell of fresh water spraying past my face. Of course, there was also the unmistakable aroma of exhaust from the boat engine floating in the air past my nose. I made it all the way around the lake that day, hanging on for dear life before letting go of the rope right in front of the camp. I landed with a rather ungraceful splash, about one hundred yards from shore, but I was triumphant. I had conquered those narrow slats of mahogany atop the shimmering waters of the lake.

At the time, the biggest sense of pride came from my ability to hang on to that rope, while being pulled behind Al's boat with him driving. After all, Al was the speed demon of the skiing world. I'm sure he didn't pull me with the throttle wide open that day since it was my first time on skis, but it felt like he had. That always was a great source of joy in Al's life, to pull skiers with the "pedal to the metal," going lickety-split with the wind blowing his thinning hair, and the water occasionally spraying his face when a wave would splash across the bow. His cigarette dangled from his mouth as he rode the open waves in his captain's hat. His jeans were always rolled up to his knees with blue, deck shoes like Gilligan wore on the deserted island. Al actually hated the water—that is—getting into the water. Only once did I ever see him get wet above his knees. That just wasn't in his bucket list of things to do. Yet, he loved to ride the waves in his boat, the pride and joy of his life. Being the captain of his boat on the water was his escape, his freedom; it was the release that made his summer special. If he had been born a hundred years earlier, I'm sure he would have spent his time sailing on the open seas. He looked like an old deck hand. Tall and wiry, he was as skinny as a rail. He could have easily merged with the sea. In fact, given the opportunity, he could have easily been the inspiration for Hemingway's book, "*The Old Man and the Sea*."

As I walked up to the shore, trudging through the miry muck of the lake bottom, skimming the skis along the water behind me, Tim came running out to greet me with a congratulatory high-five. I began to exuberantly share the experience with him, providing insight, advice on the things to do, as well as, the things not to do. Within minutes I had gone from a complete novice skier, to an expert with immeasurable experience. It was time to start preparing Tim for his journey through the treacherous waters of the skiing world. I didn't want him to go out unprepared into those shark, well, at least, carp-infested waters. I didn't want him to get caught with his guard down in those deep murky waters where danger lurked beneath the surface. I knew it wouldn't be long before he gave it a good old college try, because he wasn't about to let me do something that he couldn't. In that respect we had our rivalries as we each challenged the other. We both dared to go beyond our limits to see what we were capable of — to see if we could do something that the other hadn't yet conquered. It wasn't a pride thing at all. We never held any of those things over the head of the other. Really, it was a matter of testing our limits, then encouraging the other to conquer it, too. Within that rivalry, that conquering spirit, we developed a closeness, a bond as we continuously encouraged one another to stretch our abilities to go to the next level. Tim skied for the first time that weekend, too. He did just like I did. He fell down, and then got back in the saddle again, ready to get up out of the water to make his way all around the lake. I don't think that Al and Lea had any idea at the time that they had just created a couple of young, skiing monsters!

From that moment on, we skied whenever no one else was in line to go. We would ski eight or nine times a day; sometimes by ourselves, but more often than not, we skied together. There were also many times that Randy, or Billee, or Danny, once he started skiing, would all go together. At least once a weekend, all five of us were skiing together on that sparkling, greenish-blue water of that prairie reservoir. Several times we cleared all the boaters off the lake as our little group of merry skiers circled the lake with, not four or five or even six skiers behind the boat, but with ten skiers skiing behind Al's little cruiser. All the other boaters kindly provided an extra-wide berth as they pulled their vessels onto the shore, grabbed their cameras to get a shot of this unique sight, as if it were right out of the act of Florida's Cyprus Gardens' skiing escapades. The local Rangers even took some pictures of this strange odyssey, which they later displayed on the Marina bulletin board. Times like these were one of the highlights of our summer adventures as one big happy family!

In retrospect, it really wasn't all the adventures during those finite days of summer that make them so memorable. It was sharing life together, feeling the exhilaration of the wind, the mist of the wake's spray as they engulfed you with a refreshing coolness on a hot summers' day. The elements, along with the contentment of relationship, filled your senses on trips around the lake. There is nothing more relaxing than basking in the sun's radiant warmth as you gently float uninhibited on an inner tube that sways in time with the gentle rolling waves of surf lapping into shore. We spent endless hours riding inner tubes, standing on inner tubes, diving from inner tubes, even skiing off of inner tubes so we didn't have to get wet. There were endless games of water football along the shoreline, with Frisbee, horseshoe tossing, swimming contests, playing mud bombers, snorkeling, seeing who could hold their breath the longest, even midnight swims that were illuminated by the stars above and the flickering campfire on the shore.

After those midnight swims, we would race to the fire, hastily grabbing a dry towel in an effort to dry off before dying from exposure to the cool, moon-drenched night. We would squeeze between the adults who were gathered around the fire in lounge chairs enjoying a special camaraderie. Constant chatter sprang out of those gatherings. There were plenty of jokes, stories, and a few fish tales. Beach towels were clenched tight in blue-knuckled fists, tightly wrapped around our shoulders with goose bumps popping out like mosquito bites all over our shivering bodies as we drew close to the warmth emanating from the coals of the fire. The water dripped off of our swimming suits, creating a puddle of lake water beneath us in the fire-warmed sand.

After finally warming up, one of our moms would head up to the campers to bring back an adequate supply of marshmallows and the necessary roasting wires. We would kick back to try our hand at roasting the perfect marshmallow. There's an art involved in the preparation and creation of the perfect marshmallow. It's a learned skill, one that takes practice, as well as a great deal of patience. The perfect marshmallow is one that is completely golden brown without a trace of black or charcoal on the crispy outer shell. None of us actually preferred eating these tasty treats that way, because it really is all about the taste, the texture, the unadulterated pleasure that comes from adorning one's self with this sugary, sticky cream de stick. The true marshmallow connoisseur doesn't care if marshmallows are golden brown, slightly charcoaled, or even burnt to a delicate crunch; it's all about enjoying the unforgettable flavor that was created in the hottest coals of a flickering campfire. However, there is no challenge in toasting them just for the enjoyment of a sticky treat. The challenge that motivated us involved the challenge (as well as a bit of pride involving showing off just a bit to all the crowd) that you possessed the skill, the ability, the creative genius necessary to patiently manipulate the infamous "marshmallow wire" like a confectionary rotisserie.

We grew up together, as a family. Randy, Danny, Billee, Tim and I shared a closeness that very few people ever experience in life. We seldom fought on any of those trips. After all, our parents had no tolerance for such things. We shared nearly magical times together on those ski trips that continued on for over a decade. There was endless fun, good times, and I couldn't even begin to describe how amazing all of the food was. Every day at the lake was a smorgasbord of the finest camping cuisine. Those times provided a means of growing up that allowed us to bond both emotionally and spiritually as our bodies matured into adults. The times spent together during the summers at the lake provided the catalyst of companionship that would last for a lifetime. I don't know how our folks did it week after week during those summer months. The amount of work before and after each trip was enough to fill most work weeks.

Of course, it wasn't like this was the only interest that boys enjoyed during the days of summer. Randy, Danny and I were all deeply involved in the greatest of all America's pastimes, "baseball." We had either games or practices every day of the week. What compounded that parental concern was that we were each on different teams. With all of our games and practices at different times throughout the day and evening, it required a serious juggling act for the folks. Just the job of shuttling us around would be enough to drive most parents completely nuts. But, Mom and Dad also found the time to attend nearly every one of our games. Not only did they attend those games as a sign of support to us, but they also had a pretty significant fondness for the sport.

From the time any of us were walking, we had a bat and ball in our hands. We inherited a genetic link for the game from Grandpa Williams, who always took the time to teach every "boy" child in the family the intricacies of the sport. His eyes would glisten with delight as he shared stories of his bygone days, as he participated with his own small town team that traveled from town to town to challenge each other for regional bragging rights. Of course, I'm sure there was always a bit of friendly wagering going on too between the players to make the games a bit more interesting. Grandpa could never sit on the sidelines to watch a Sunday afternoon makeshift game between family siblings. Once we'd drag out the bats and balls, before you knew it, he would be out in the yard, kneeling down on his knees on a makeshift pitcher's mound, ensuring that every child had their chance at a hit-able pitch. You could never strike out as long as Grandpa was on the mound. He made sure that you went down hitting the ball. So, with the love of baseball instilled in our hearts, on almost every one of those trips to the lake, before the sun would set behind the distant horizon, the bats and balls would come out as sides would be chosen for the challenge.

Even though it was a lot of work to get ready for those trips, we were all expected to pitch in. After all, there would always be plenty of time for relaxing, with lots of laughing, conversing, and camaraderie during those weekend getaways. There was a contentment that accompanied those times at the lake. Maybe that came from the quiet walks along the beach as the sun slowly set beyond the rolling hills with its rainbow of fluorescent hues that glistened off the reflecting water. I loved those moments when we were afforded an amazing example of our parents walking hand in hand along the water's edge as the waves gently lapped beneath their feet. Growing up in a loving, caring family, witnessing what it means to give of yourself—to share with others—was a key to successful parenting. As I sit back to reflect on those days, I feel the Lord provided me with a near-perfect childhood. The earthly family that I was born into was as perfect as humanly possible. Of course, we had our problems and quirks, but I wouldn't trade my family for anything in this world.

One of the funniest incidents that happened at the lake occurred one year when Tim and I were about sixteen. The previous year, both of our families, along with Lea and Al, had taken a trip to Lake Powell in Arizona. Uncle Don had rented a boat for the day, and to his misfortune, it was the last one available so he chose to go ahead to take a chance on it. It really wasn't much of a ski boat, it looked more like an old, converted fishing boat that someone had thrown a coat of paint on and then slapped a makeshift windshield over its bow. It had a small outboard motor but the seats were just wooden slats that stretched from one side of the boat to the other. It was a terrible experience to take that under-powered dingy out onto the vastness of

Lake Powell. Plus it was pretty embarrassing for Don to putt along at full throttle trying to keep up with Dad's boat.

Don's humiliation was probably the deciding factor in purchasing his own boat the next spring. Well, the boat he decided to buy wasn't too much bigger than the one he had rented at Powell. However, this one was actually designed as a ski boat, although maybe it was designed to pull the munchkins from Oz on skis. It was a used boat, about fourteen-feet long with an 80-horse engine. We hadn't seen his new toy until they pulled in that day. Don was pretty excited to launch it in an attempt to get his feet wet as a boat owner. Well, maybe that's not the best analogy. Once it was in the water, his little craft looked smaller than ever. It sat pretty low in the water, especially after a 220-pound Uncle Don and a dainty (I can't divulge her true weight) Aunt Dorothy climbed aboard. Tim and I quickly volunteered to serve as the inaugural skiing guinea pigs. Actually, we all skied for quite a while. Surprisingly, the boat did a pretty fair job of pulling us even though it wasn't as big or near as powerful as Dad's boat. (I know, it sounds like one of those, "My boat is bigger than your boat," stories.)

After skiing for most of the morning, Uncle Don came roaring in with the engine screaming toward the sandy shore. He was standing at the helm with his vivid farmer's tan adorning his shirtless physique as he peered above the windshield. You could see the pride beaming across his face underneath that weather-worn straw hat that had become his trademark. He was carefully guiding his craft into a pre-selected sandy berth as he pulled back on the throttle to glide in the remainder of the way without power, when something totally unexpected happened. The wake behind the boat caught up with the slowing vessel, allowing the water to come crashing over the back of the motor, flooding the boat. With the weight of his passengers, combined with the weight of the incoming water, the low-riding boat began to go down. Like the Titanic on that fateful night, Don's little dingy was about to take the final plunge. They were about 50 yards off shore when Don started screaming for help. We all rushed out to grab any part of the boat that was still above water, and tugging with all our might, we frantically towed her into the shore. Don was quite the sight, standing at the helm, with his straw hat shading his eyes, and also, holding in the rising temperature of his boiling wrath and humbled pride.

Some of us towed, while others grabbed buckets to begin bailing water. Don steered her in like a true captain, begrudgingly going down with the ship. Fortunately, we got her into the shallow water before the keel settled into the sand. We were close enough to shore that water didn't continue to rise over her bulkheads. As we continued to bail water in an attempt to dry out the hull-thing, we began to laugh at the narrowly diverted disaster. Actually, it really was quite funny. The only real damage was to Don's ego. We quickly discovered though, that we needed to keep our smirks and snickers to ourselves, since Don didn't seem to find any humor in the situation. Before this mishap at sea, none of us had ever seen Don mad. He was usually the good humor man, but this event proved to be the exception, as he was as mad as a hornet. Don was furious to the core, not taking kindly to being the brunt of our jokes.

Mom had been standing on the shore, taking pictures of the whole episode as the rest of us frantically pulled the sinking craft to the shore. Actually, she was the one who started off with some ill-placed humorous rhetoric. With her quick wit, she quickly discovered Don was not going to be the butt of everyone's jokes as he climbed out of the boat to head up for some solitary reflection in the stinky old outhouse. So, with Don being out of earshot, the one-liners flew out like a fish after a fly. "Good thing he didn't sink a lot of money into this thing!" "It could be that he 'plunged' himself into a bad investment." "Looks like he's 'immersed' himself in misery." "Can't believe the used boat salesman 'soaked' him like that." "He looks pretty tired now, especially after being 'swamped.'" "He gives new meaning to getting 'down' to the bottom of the problem." "Ah, I'm sure he thinks that we're all 'wet!'" "Life's a 'beach' and then you 'sink.'" Yep, we had a pretty good time at Don's expense. A good time that is, until he got back down to the shore and with one "stern" look, we knew that he wasn't going to tolerate any more jokes. However, there was a silver lining to this story—the next weekend when we all gathered for another outing of sun-basked fun, Don had a sparkling new boat.

Actually, Don really was quite the character. He was always joking and laughing in that big brouhaha kind of way. He'd chuckle, then snort with a high-pitched tenor chortle whenever he'd do something that he thought was funny, regardless if anybody else would laugh along. There were times when he'd do something to Dorothy, just to hear her holler, so he could let a boisterous laugh. Dorothy would yell at him before reaching out to slug him in whatever part of his body was closest. He always used his laugh to his advantage, figuring nobody could get too mad over anything he said or did if he was laughing.

One day we were skiing while Lea was driving the boat with Mom riding along. Don was adorned with a stylish, green-and-black-striped swimsuit that went from his waist all the way down to his ankles. It was the kind that was fashioned after those worn during the nineteen-twenties. You know, the roaring twenties. He was skiing along jumping back and forth across the wake when he caught an edge of the ski. As he fell, he did his patented swan dive. He would put his hands together over his head to take the plunge in a less painful and more graceful manner. Well, when Lea circled the boat around toward him, he yelled out that his swimming suit had fallen off with the plunge and he needed a towel. There weren't any towels in the boat, so he told them that he would just have to get in since he couldn't be skiing around the lake without a swimming suit. These fine church ladies let out a squeal as they turned their backs in blushing embarrassment when he threw his swimming suit into the boat before he crawled in himself. They were both ready to punch his lights out as he walked up to the front of the boat, plopping down beside them wearing the swimming suit he was wearing underneath the old fashioned one that had come off. I've often wondered, which one of those fine, reserved ladies was the first to take a peek as they realized Don was up to his normal, twisted pranks. As Tim and I were standing in waist-deep water, waiting to be the next to ski, we could hear the ladies shrieks all the way to shore. That is, we could hear their shrieks until they were drowned out by Don's hysterical cackle of a laugh. He laughed about that one for hours, walking around the camp all day with a smirk of contentment pompously emblazoned across his face.

It didn't matter where Don went, what you saw was what you got with him. Whether he was at a church social, a Bible study, in his own backyard, or out at the lake, he was always full of mischief. He was the proverbial prankster. An aggravation, just waiting to happen, although he was a fun aggravation to watch. If he wasn't pinching Dorothy on the backside, as a means to completely aggravate her, he would be off picking some old farmer's corn in the fields that surrounded the lake. He never cared if it was field corn or sweet corn, we often had the treat of corn picked fresh from the field with one of our meals at the lake—that is if it was the end of the summer and the corn was ripe for the pickin'. After all, he was pretty particular about the corn he "borrowed" as he would refer to it. He wouldn't think about picking any if it wasn't in season. "The farmers got a whole field full," he'd say, "They'll never miss a dozen ears."

There were many a time when he'd come back from the outhouses that were scattered around the lake, joking about the reflection of the big old fat lady he saw while taking care of his business up on the hill. He always referred to those outdoor toilets as the house of "mirrors." You always wanted to keep the lid down on the stool if you were changing clothes in there since the waters below provided a pretty clear view of the person on the other side. I must admit, that as a young teenager whose hormones were starting to flow exponentially, I used to accompany Tim up to those grungy, grotesque-smelling port-a-pots to try to catch a glimpse of any pretty girls who happened to wander in. You had to look quick though, as the smells, along with the flies were so bad that you had to hold your breath any time you were closer than fifty feet to those outdoor cesspools. We never camped too close to those places either because of the rank odor, along with all the pesky bugs. In fact, not only could you smell them from a mile away, it sounded like a squadron of B-52 bombers flying overhead from all the flies, gnats, and mosquitos buzzing around. Even when it was pitch black at night, the only senses you needed to find the place to take care of your business was your nose and ears, flashlights were never necessary. That's why it was always a nice little hike up to the house of sweet relief. Of course, you never wanted to wait too long before the call of nature turned into a full-blown emergency run.

It's hard to admit that there is a lustful desire inside everyone. Tim and I were no exception, although I'm sure all males possess that tendency to a much higher degree. I even remember Dad saying on a few occasions, after being caught by Mom as he ogled an entourage of bikini-clad ladies, "It doesn't hurt to look!"

But, all the girls who used those outhouses were just as aware of their reflective qualities as the boys were. Why, we actually saw more skin on the beach with those bikini-clad babes than we ever did in the house of mirrors. One of those embarrassing moments happened when we got caught by Al as we were hanging around the reflecting pool like a couple of vultures waiting for their prey to die. Tim was inside when this cute girl walked into the ladies' side to change out of her bikini. "Hey, Lanny, come in here to check this out!" he whispered, just as Al walked up beside me. Al stood behind Tim, whispering over his shoulder, "What do you see?" Tim just about shot through the cement roof of that outhouse. We both shot out of there like a bolt of lightning, with our feet barely touching the ground as we jetted our way back to camp. Al never told anybody about our little adventure, at least as far as I know. We did spend the rest of the weekend, though, keeping a pretty low profile. But as I think about it, I can't remember Al coming back to the camp too soon after our arrival. Who knows what he was really up to? I'm sure that Lea would have given him an earful if she thought he had been up to checking out the reflective scenery. Maybe that's why he never mentioned it to anybody. No matter though, I can still see Al smiling from ear to ear as he walked in on Tim, catching us in the act of one of those Deadly Sins. In fact, I'm sure this was Deadly Sin Number Six of childhood, "Never sneak around spying on thy neighbor for lustful purposes." Which of course can lead to the breaking of several of the biblical commandments, as covetous desires can soon lead to adulterous behavior.

Life on the lake also had its down sides. Besides the afternoon winds, accompanied by some pretty severe thunderstorms, it seemed that the bugs, mosquitoes, and horseflies were always biting. There was never enough repellent around to keep the bugs at bay for any extended amount of time. And of course, sand infiltrated everything, creeping into every wrinkle and crevice, finding its way between your toes and into your sleeping bag and your swimming suit, as well as your hair and scalp. Somehow it seemed to find its way into the food too, which, I suppose might have helped the digestive tract by adding a bit more fiber.

Showers were non-existent when we were at the lake. If you wanted to clean-up, you had to rinse off in the lake, or take a spit bath with a wash rag using a basin of water. If you were really serious though, you could take your shampoo or soap with you in the lake and lather up. Dorothy was always after us to stay out of the mud in an effort to stay semi-clean. But, when they started draining the water out of the lake for irrigating the farms around the county, the shore turned into a twelve-inch-deep mud bog. Staying clean was next to impossible for two boys. Getting to the water was like walking through a tar pit. With every step, the strength required to pull your foot out of the thick goo was like trying to walk through a batch of twenty-year-old molasses.

One of the cool, macho things that all of us did as we came in from a skiing trip around the lake was to try to get as close to the shore as possible so that the water from our ski wouldn't come up over the back of our head to soak us. However, with this "look at how great of a skier I am trick," there was always the possibility of getting too close to the shore, causing the ski fin to stick in the sand, which knocked you flat on your face in ankle-deep water. All of us had done it once or twice, and it defeated the purpose of practicing a beach start, which allowed the skier to step off in knee-deep water so you never really got wet. The beach start, or "jerking off," as we used to call it before that phrase took on a different connotation, literally was quite the athletic feat. You would walk out to knee-deep water, coil up about ten feet of slack in the tow rope, and when the boat pulls out at full throttle, all the slack is quickly pulled taut allowing you to just step up on the ski like you're stepping onto a porch. Away you go, at full speed, appearing like the most amazing professional skier on this watery planet. After mastering this technique, Randy, Danny, Tim and I never skied any other way. Not only was it the coolest way to start, but it always impressed all of the bikini-clad girls who happened to be within eyeshot of the shoreline.

"Stepping off" became the fad for everyone in our weekend skiing warrior band. (Even Mom and Dorothy finally mastered the technique.) It didn't matter who was skiing together with two or even three other skiers behind the boat, we'd take advantage of the coolest of all ways to start our collective trips around the lake. If you'd do it right, not only did you not get wet above your knees, but you also were the beneficiary of quite the adrenaline rush. "Stepping off" felt like you were being shot out of a canon when the tow rope became taut and you stepped up on the top of the crystal waters of the lake. However, if you didn't do it right, there was the chance that you would do a face-plant in knee-deep water. More times than not, that would definitely leave a mark or possibly, two!

One day, after they had started draining the lake to irrigate the farmer's fields, Dorothy went skiing, "stepping off" with impeccable style on her customary one ski. It was a start worthy of the cover of a "*Sports Illustrated*" edition. She gracefully made her trip around the lake with a swimming suit that was as dry as if it had been on the clothesline all afternoon. Not wanting to get wet on the landing, she decided to let go of the rope as close to the shore as possible. Al, being at the helm, and, as always, driving like there was no tomorrow, brought the boat screaming in toward the shore, just like always, as he was intent on giving each skier an accelerated thrill at the end of their trip. Well, this time, he must have given the throttle a little extra punch, because when Dorothy let go of the rope, she shot out of the boat's wake like a tornado whipping through a trailer park. She screamed all the way to the shore with her arms flapping like a "blue-footed booby" bird trying to land. The tip of her ski wiggled wildly out of control as the ski chattered across the tops of the lapping waves heading into the shore. Fortunately, for her, she remembered those profound words of wisdom about keeping her mouth shut just as the fin on the bottom of the ski dug in to the miry lake bottom as her screaming ride came to an abrupt halt. She did a face-plant in the twelve-inch deep, thick, oozing, black, foul-smelling, lake bottom mud. Total silence filled the air when only moments before her spine-tingling screams of horror had permeated the lake front.

Mom, who had been watching Dorothy's landing from the comfort of the camper doorway, screamed out for Dad to go rescue his sister. Dad jumped out of his lounge chair with a burst of adrenaline as he ran toward the shore line, looking everywhere for any sign of his older sibling. He looked like a drunken sailor as he staggered around in total desperation searching for his sister. "Where is she?" he kept yelling out.

When he finally made his way to the lake's edge, he nearly ran her over as his grotesque, swamp-monster-of-a-sister arose from the miry bed covered with the stinking, sticky, thick, black lake bottom dripping from her unrecognizable form. She was covered from head to toe as she raised her arms straight out from her shoulders, flinging the grimy slime, or at least trying to fling it all off. The only color other than that of the black mud that was visible on her, were the whites of her eyes and teeth, as she stood there completely immersed in the most complete mudpack ever known in the spa world. Literally, she looked as if she was part of an "*I Love Lucy*" episode as she stood there not knowing whether to laugh or cry. Of course, none of us helped the matter, after realizing she was alright, at least physically, we all broke out in total hysterics. Really, it wasn't just a good laugh, but one of those times you get a stitch in your side from laughing so hard, and you can't even stay standing as you fall on your knees, or back into a chair with uncontrolled laughter. Unfortunately, it all happened so fast nobody had time to grab a camera. Just our luck too, as Tim always regretted not having a picture of her in that state so he could proudly show his friends what his loving "mudder" really looked like without makeup. It did help our cause though, as she never got after either one of us again for playing in the mud or getting messy.

Everyone in our exclusive little skiing community enjoyed the actual sport of donning a pair of skis to jet across the water, everyone, except Al. He was the designated driver, adopting my younger brother Danny as his first mate—that is, until Danny got too big to sit on his lap to drive the boat. Starting at the tender age of six, Danny would hop in the boat, put on Al's captain's hat to "man" the helm. That's probably why Danny still likes to live on the edge to ski faster than any of the rest of us. He learned from the master of the skiing speed demon. Al really did help instill in him a love of the water that later on inspired Danny to venture into the undersea world of scuba diving. He eventually became an instructor.

Lea and Al had a round, plywood saucer that was about three feet in circumference. Dad would use that old board almost like a set of skis as Danny and Al would drive the boat, while dad performed his wide array of watery tricks and antics. Dad would go backward on that thing, spin around like a top, jump the boat wakes with it, and at times he'd even take along an old canvas camp stool to sit on it while he was in tow behind Al's boat. Dad's use of that saucer was the only way we could get Al to slow down, since the maximum speed to safely handle the thing was about 15 miles per hour. Dad got to the point where that's really all he ever wanted to do, other than drive his own boat to pull skiers.

It was quite the sight to see Dad out on that saucer, spinning around, going sideways, or even backward as he held the rope behind his back. Often times, he would start spinning around on it so many times that he got to a point he was too dizzy to even stand up. I think his record was 36 spins without ever stopping. He used to take Danny along with him on the circular board; that is, before Danny was able to ski on his own. He really did master that thing and about the only thing he didn't do while on that board was stand on his head. He took our little Pomeranian dog, Cookie, with him a time or two for a trip around the lake. It was always funny to watch Dad carry Cookie out to the water for a ride-along. As soon as Cookie got close to the water, his four little legs frantically went into doggie-paddle mode. It was a great way to give that little furball a bath, and as soon as the ride was over, Dad would throw him in the boat to dry off. Tim and I both tried our luck on the saucer, quickly discovering that going around in circles was not our cup of tea. I never did like getting too dizzy. I never spun around more than thirteen times before taking a plunge into the watery abyss. After a few attempts of mastering that old saucer, I quickly decided to leave the trickery to the real master, Dad, and I would stick to slalom skiing, which suited me much better.

Spending nearly every weekend of the summer at the lake was a great way to grow up. Nothing can compare to the smell of a day along the lakeshore. The fragrance of suntan lotion; the scent of sage, along with ragweed being blown across the water by a gentle summer breeze; the moss and algae that cover the shoreline as the waves wash themselves back into the lake from which they came; the noxious smell of gasoline from the boats, along with the stinging, pungent foulness from the blue-smoke exhaust escaping from the back of the boat engines; the aroma of grasses and wildflowers, of cottonwood trees, and insect spray; of drying lake sand mixed with the water-saturated muds that throw off a distinct stench of their own; the scent of fishy waters, along with an occasional whiff of a rotting carp washed up along the shoreline. Yes, those were the aromas of the lake that instantly bring back sweet memories hidden deep within the recesses of my heart and mind.

The trips to the various lakes in Colorado provided an opportunity to experience the outdoors, to appreciate the natural resources, and to respect the bountiful riches that God has blessed us with in this country. Life on the lake allowed us to bond as a family, rely on each other to play together, and rely on each other to take care of chores required within the experience of those recreational times. It didn't matter whether it was loading or unloading the boats, helping get the meals together or putting them out on the picnic tables, or even helping to clean up the meals by doing the dishes, it was a family affair when everybody had to pitch in. Everybody helped when it was time to pitch a tent, set up camp, or pack things up to go home. There were also times when everyone in camp frantically scurried about in an effort to batten down the hatches to secure all of our belongings when an afternoon thunderstorm suddenly burst through the camp, while scattering our belongings across the lakeshore. Many times, those storms seemed like tornadoes wreaking havoc on anything that wasn't tied down, and a few times, even some of the items that were. More than once we had to scurry out to the lakeshore in order to secure one of the boats that had come loose in the midst of a mighty wind storm. During times like that, it was all-hands-on-deck to make sure the boats weathered the storm with no damage.

There really was something magical about those days on those Colorado lakes. In retrospect they seem almost like a dream. There was something beyond special about them that can never be repeated or found again in this life. They can only be relived within the confines of my memory. Maybe they were really attributable to the unfettered fun of childhood. It is possible life's magical moments are best witnessed through the eyes of a child. I often wonder if the realities of life in the adult world aren't tarnished by responsibility or the struggles we face. Maybe our eyes become clouded because of the injustice or trials that constantly attack us. But then again, maybe the days we shared together as a family at the lake really were touched by summer's magic!

One of the most memorable outings we ever enjoyed as a family occurred during the first vacation we went on to Lake Powell. This reservoir, which stretches for more than 180 miles behind the Glenn Canyon Dam at Page, Arizona is in my mind one of the seven wonders of the United States. The lake encompasses more than 1,800 miles of shoreline in one of the most pristine canyon lands of America. Its waters are supplied by the Colorado River as it snakes a path through parts of Utah, and winds into Arizona. It originates in the Rocky Mountains of Colorado, coming from the melted snow of the majestic peaks of the western slope. The water-filled canyon lands provide a breathtaking beauty that can only be found within the confines of the western United States.

As you travel through these immense canyons with their tall sandstone cliffs, along with the multi-colored rock formations that tower hundreds of feet above the water's surface, you can relate to the awestruck wonder that explorer John Wesley Powell and his men must have experienced during their expedition to the West. As they traveled through the swift-moving Colorado River in their small wooden vessels, on their way to the California coast hundreds of years earlier, they must have been nearly overwhelmed at the beauty, as well as the enormity of this land. The earth-tone colors that stain the sides of the giant cliffs and bluffs are a reminder of the colors of the rainbow; reds, yellows, gold, dark green, and deep purples that are nearly black, bleed down the face of the jagged canyon walls. Those sandstone formations contain an entire spectrum of color that seems to change with the time of day as the rays of the sun radiate across the peaks, illuminating the valleys, while casting a radiant shadow across the ever-changing landscape.

This land was home to members of the Anasazi Indian tribe, who existed peacefully with their crops, living off the land nearly fifteen-hundred years before our modern age. Their existence is evidenced everywhere you look along the canyon walls and tributaries that drain into the main channel of the canyon. Pictographs, the stories of native lives, can be found among the overhanging walls and indentations of the land. Their ghost-like images were painted with painstaking care by artists who wanted to leave a personal mark or legacy upon the landscape so that their story would carry on for future generations to interpret. Stories of the hardships associated with the eking out of a meager existence. They depict a long-forgotten way of life, which included the types of crops they grew, the foods they ate, and, of course, depictions of animals they hunted. These images provide a glimpse into life, as well as portraits of the unavoidable death that hovers over each of us. Through their drawings, we can feel the hope they had for a better life, as they struggled to survive in this harsh, barren wilderness. These original native occupants left their mark on this arid, desert region. It's a land that can reach temperatures nearing 120-degrees during the height of the summer day, with evening temperatures that drop to chill your bones. This land was home to lizards, snakes, and scorpions. Its sparse vegetation of grass, yuccas, an occasional scrub oak or pinion tree provided nourishment and cover for the smallest of God's creatures. Its ability to sustain much life, outside of a few rabbits, squirrels or coyotes was nearly non-existent.

Anasazi dwellings still littered the canyon walls, nestled snugly along the top rim of a cliff, protected by an overhanging ledge of sandstone. They were nearly impossible to see from the canyon floor below unless caught by a trained eye looking specifically for a row of rocks that seemed lined up a bit too perfectly to be naturally made. These dwellings were a monument to a civilization that had once passed through this region, suddenly vanishing without a trace. Walking through those ruins with a slight breeze rustling my hair, as the hot sun beat down on my shoulders, made me think how they once hustled and bustled with activity. These ruins were home to families, with children, where babies were born under the careful eye of multi-generations. Grandparents were an integral part of each family, where they passed down their skills, wisdom and folklore to a brood of children, eager to learn about the "good ole days." Here in these clay-brick dwellings with their wood and mud roofs, people lived, and as life goes, people died.

There was an overwhelming sense of sanctity in those dwellings as I gingerly walked the grounds with images of distant cultures dancing through my mind. I was walking where a nearly forgotten civilization dealt with the challenges of life. Men and women, who laughed, cried; who hurt, bled; who struggled and fought with the problems of the day, necessary to just stay alive. A people who also had hopes and dreams for living, along with maintaining their own way of life. Maybe they dreamed of building a new addition for their mother-in-law, or maybe they were constantly on the lookout for the perfect piece of flint to craft a new knife to more efficiently skin an animal that was killed to provide food and clothing for the family.

I'm sure they lifted their eyes to the heavens to see if there were any clouds on the horizon that might bring some much-needed rain to water their meager crops of corn, gourds or squash. They must have constantly been dreaming about successfully stalking their prey, in order to make the perfect shot with their primitive weapon of choice or possibly necessity. Then I'm sure that they also envisioned a triumphant return to the cliff dwelling with young children scurrying underfoot with their youthful exhilaration as fresh-killed game was carried over a strong, bronzed shoulder.

Were these people really any different than me? Or, was the only thing that separated their lives from mine based on the concept of time? Everywhere I looked, I saw a glimpse of a forgotten civilization, where real people once lived and played. There were footholds dug into the sides of the rock formations that led down to the river's edge. Occasionally, I would find a piece of flint, an arrowhead, or a small piece of pottery. Dad once found two small, shriveled up pieces of corn lying beside one of the dwellings. That was back at a time when it wasn't a federal crime to pick up an artifact. Maybe that was one of the reasons that our trips to Lake Powell were so enjoyable, they reminded me that there were people who had come this way before, not just a few years ago, but centuries and millennia ago. It brought to the forefront of my mind the fact that past civilizations, past generations, had touched my life in mysterious, unknown ways and they would continue doing so for the rest of my life.

Fishing at Lake Powell was fantastic for everybody, except me. The only kind of fish I could catch were the kind the "lollipop kids" from Oz caught—the pint-sized variety. While Al, Tim, Danny and Randy were reeling in 14- to 17-inch beauties, I was throwing back minnows, praying that maybe someday they might grow up to be a fish. Sometimes I felt like one of those minnows, wondering if I'd ever grow up to be anything other than a half-pint. It was obvious from the way fishing went that when I did make it to adulthood, I wouldn't make it as a fisherman. Mom even took a picture of me holding up my catch of the day, a four-inch perch. The picture served as a constant reminder that fishing was not one of my strong suits. Mom grabbed the camera just as I hooked what I thought was a big one. It really was putting up quite a fight, as the tip of my rod was dipping down like

I had a ten-pound catfish hooked on the end of the line. I reeled and reeled, keeping the tip of the rod up as I struggled to land this whale of a fish. Finally, after several minutes of fighting, the fish gave up the fight, allowing me to reel him to the shore. When he finally came out of the water, along with an even bigger piece of moss stuck to the old lead weight, I couldn't believe its size. If it was four inches, I was lucky, and the moss that had been the real cause of the fight was probably twice the size of the fish. I held up my rod with that little guy dangling from the line, just as Mom snapped the picture, forever cursing my ability to even tell a good fish story. After the humiliation of having photographic proof of my lack of fishing prowess, I convinced Tim and Danny to accompany me on a hike along the edge of the sand formations that jutted out along the edge of the lake.

The water at Powell is deeper than several-hundred feet in spots, and its crystal clear waters provided pristine visibility. It's one of the few places that I've been where you can look down to see your feet while treading water. Although the water's reflective qualities makes your legs appear as if they are attached to your neck. It was always fun to walk along the cliffs that were about ten to twenty feet above the water and pick up a rock to drop over the edge. Now I'm not talking about a small rock, I'm talking about the kind that took two boys and a horse to pick up and heave over the edge. We were constantly focused on finding a rock that would make an even bigger splash than the previous one. It was quite the sight to watch each rock sink down at least twenty or thirty feet before it disappeared into the dark blue abyss at the bottom of the lake.

Danny, Tim and I were walking along the edge that day trying to see if we could fill up the lake with rocks as we tossed every one that we came upon, over the edge of the cliff and into the water. We had always been warned to watch out for snakes when we were out in the wild, and at Powell, we also had to be on the lookout for scorpions too. So, as we rolled over each rock, we kept our feet at a good distance just to make sure that some reptilian creature or arthropod didn't scurry out from beneath the rock to dart up our legs.

As we continued our hike along the edge, I came upon this one, perfect rock that was shaped like an oversize discus used by the Greeks in the original Olympic games. It was about eighteen-inches long and four-inches thick with a perfect symmetry. If I were a giant, it would have been the perfect skipping stone. I reached out with my leg to give it a shove with my toes, just to make sure that nothing lived beneath it. When nothing came crawling out, I decided it was perfect for throwing off the twenty-foot cliff, down into the beautiful aqua-blue waters of the lake below. Tim and Dan excitedly leaned close to the edge of the cliff to watch me catapult this monstrosity of a rock into its watery grave. When I picked up that hefty piece of sandstone to lift it above my head, two fruit bats that had been clinging to the bottom of the rock came screeching off with their wings wildly flapping. Talk about getting out of there without our feet hitting the ground, I don't know whether the three of us hit the water before the rock did or not. It seemed like time stood still from the time we jumped off that twenty-foot cliff until we finally hit the water like cannon balls shot out of a mortar. Fortunately, we found a gentle sloping edge that we were able to swim to in order to climb out of the water and back up the cliff. But I have to admit that all three of us were a bit unnerved, and we didn't play our little game of "throw the rock off the cliff to see it splash" for the rest of that trip.

That night, we ended up having one of the best fish fries of my entire life, thanks to Al and nearly everyone else who had been fishing that day. It was by far, one of the best meals we had at the lake that year, a real fishfest, with catfish, perch, crappie, and a few monster sunfish. Unfortunately, my pint-sized minnow wasn't worth cleaning so I had nothing to contribute to the skillet cuisine. But, as my pun-filled mind looks back on that moment, I find great satisfaction in knowing that the "scales" of bad fortune had "perched" upon my shoulders, providing me with a pretty "crappie" fishing experience. However, as they say in Latin, "*carpe diem*" or seize the moment, but at least I was never a "sucker" again, as I retired my gear and cut the "bait."

There was always something to do when we were at Lake Powell. If we weren't riding down the lake in the boats, admiring the amazing scenery with its awe-inspiring splendor and majesty, we were skiing, fishing, or jumping into the warm, almost bath-like waters, cooling off from the nearly unbearable heat. We would swim for hours in a secluded cove where the sandstone rock formation gave way to an outstretched sandy beach, allowing us to land the boats. We would swim around the edges of the shore, exploring every nook, cranny and indentation of the rocks, finding shelter from the heat of the sun. Often, we would find large pieces of driftwood washed up on the shore, then pull them back out into the water to use as a floating device to leisurely relax in an outstretched position, laying just inches above the water. At times, we would climb up on the bows of the boats to jump off into the deep, refreshing waters in a competition of who could jump the farthest while staying under water the longest. When there was nothing else to do, we would float on our backs to gaze at the clouds as they swirled high above the towering cliffs that stretched up toward the deep blue, western sky. Nothing is more relaxing than floating in the water as the waves gently lap around your body. The sun rays glisten off the waters and into your squinting eyes as you bask in the unbelievable tranquility in the warmth of the day.

Powell is an immense lake. Its vastness was almost overwhelming, its beauty nearly indescribable. Tim and I skied together on the last day of our trip, for fourteen miles as we made our way back to the marina. We jumped the wake from the boat, crossed under each other's rope, and held the ropes between our knees, essentially skiing with "no" hands. We sprayed each other with the wake of our skis when we started to get hot. As we cruised along on our skis, we pointed out the awesome scenery that would catch our eye. We gracefully flew by the lake's magnificence with our skis barely skimming the surface of the waters. We totally enjoyed our time together, not only with each other, but with all of our family. I will never forget the family riding together in the boat, with Dad driving. His curly black hair flattened against his head as he peered over the windshield, guiding us through the watery maze of the lake's canyons.

Dad loved to drive his boat. Just like Al, his boat was his pride. He had served in the Navy for four years aboard a Destroyer, the *USS Twining*. He served as a machinist mate in the ship's engine room during the Korean War. The sea was in his blood. His boat provided him a taste of his Navy days. It brought back memories of his many adventures from his younger years as the wind, the mist, and the sun kissed his face. He often shared those memories with us, which added to our joy of boating. Those stories allowed me to imagine the way things had once been, and enhanced my own ability to dream.

Our parents invested a vast amount of energy, resources, time and money into those boating trips. Of course, they also enjoyed the trips, but I think the big motivating factor was wanting to do things together as a family. They instilled in us the importance of family, of being there for each other. All of us became better people because of that investment. The times we shared boating, skiing, fishing and relaxing were truly magical. The days were enchanting as the weather blanketed us with its peaceful demeanor, as well as its relentless torrent. The nights overflowed with an almost mystical existence as the stars, the moon, the galaxy encompassed us with a glistening, gentle radiance. On those nights it felt as if you could feel the hands of God gently caressing you. As a child, my heart was filled with never-ending love and security. I felt as if there was not a care in the world. I felt protected from evil when I was surrounded by the people that I loved so dearly. We were like one big, happy family where everybody looked after each other. The closeness, the bond that developed between all of us on those carefree summer days on the water can never be severed. Contained within those days of summer's magic, our lives were sprinkled with the effervescence of love and tranquility. Wherever life would take us, whatever direction we would follow, there would always be in our hearts a piece of that enchanted magic that bound us together during those carefree days of summer.

The sun does rise, the sun does set, the moon shines bright at night;
    God saw the "day" that He had made, and knew that it was right . . .
Magical days, mystical days, hours filled with fun,
    Water sports and rivalries, reflections in the sun.
Camping days, skiing days, days lived on the lake,
    Boating, fishing, swimming, a great childhood this does make!
Happy days, sun-drenched days, exploring nature's joys,
    Days of roaming o'er the hills, proclaim the ways of boys.
Mountains, lakes and rivers, all playgrounds wonderful,
    Yet always special to the heart, was Grandpa's fishin' hole.
Blissful days together, finding treasures by the droves:
    An Indian piece, a pretty rock, lacy sea shells in the coves.
Horny toads and pollywogs, and lots of other things;
    Rattles from a rattlesnake, Gossamer butterfly wings.
Days of finding things to do, "I'll race you back and then,
    We'll gather eggs for Grandma, Chase the chickens 'round the pen."
Lazy days, leisure days, day dreams may come true;
    Each day is greeted with a grin, there is so much to do!
Vacation days, Lake Powell days, the high-light of July,
    Majestic scenes, breathtaking sights, beneath the deep blue sky.
Exploring days, fast-paced days, with never enough time,
    The days pass by too quickly, pleasure reaches heights sublime.
Days of close togetherness, enwrapped in "family love,"
    A boyhood life of happiness, a blessing from above . . .

—Clarice D. Cook

CHAPTER 5

They Shipped Us Off to Church Camp

Two summers in a row Tim and I went to Church Camp for a week at a time. The first time we took off for our mountain adventure was, by far, one of the most inspirational weeks of our lives. We reveled in five days of non-stop action, devotion, and exhilarating competition. Looking back, we were engulfed in a spiritually charged week of Olympic proportions. Besides that, the ultimate benefit involved meeting and hanging out with other teenagers, including girls without our parents or siblings looking over our shoulders.

The camp was located outside Bailey, Colorado, nestled among the tall, ponderosa pine trees of the Rocky Mountains and was appropriately named Id-Ra-Ha-Je, an iconic representation of George Beverly Shea's classical song, *I'd Rather Have Jesus*! The camp encompassed what seemed like hundreds of acres of God's most pristine country and boasted a variety of kid-friendly rustic accommodations, ranging from teepees to cabins and a main lodge. A unique attribute of the various camping areas was that the cabins and the teepee villages were hidden from the main lodge where we resided for our week-long adventure.

A big meadow just outside the main lodge played host to myriad games and activities that completely occupied our 120-hour retreat. The meadow provided a vast playing field for games of red rover, softball, volleyball, hoppity-hop kickball, relay races and capture-the-flag. The dirt road that circled the meadow was about a mile around and served as a boundary between the high school lodge, and the adolescent teepee village. Every morning around 6:30 a.m. we would gather outside of the main lodge to start the day with a robust rendition of calisthenics, culminating in a nice little jaunt around the mile-long drive. This little physical ritual served several purposes. First, it got us out of bed and our blood flowing. Second, it gave the kitchen staff enough time to finish breakfast preparations. Finally, it gave counselors time for coffee—a caffeinated jumpstart for keeping up with a horde of energetic teens.

Church Camp was one of those unforgettable experiences that took a bunch of immature, gangly, clumsy kids, and set them on the road toward adulthood. I know it sounds weird, but as I look back at my youth, the experience at camp was like a dividing line that clearly distinguishes my childhood days from growing into a man. I can't explain it; I'm not sure whether it was a time of realization that girls were pretty special creations, or whether it was the realization that there was more to life than games and childhood adventures. Maybe it involved the process of growing up, since it was the first time I had ever really been out of the direct supervision of parents or grandparents. I was also thrown into 120 hours of forced interaction with a bunch of kids whom I didn't know and had never met.

Tim and I would have never gone to camp by ourselves, since we were both a bit shy. Neither of us were social butterflies like the older siblings in our family. But, together, we were able to sprout wings, meet new people, make lots of friends, and venture out on an adventure of our own making. In the process, we were also beneficiaries of a spiritual awakening that would forever change our lives, and our destinies.

Our first year of camp, we were almost fifteen years old, and we accompanied our youth group from our church. We were chaperoned by Pastor Bob and his wife Lois who also organized that year's camp. I'm pretty sure that everyone, if they've spent any amount of time going to church, has had a Pastor Bob in their lives. If not, I have to feel sorry for them. Bob was a young, highly energetic minister who took pride in his Italian heritage. He played the guitar, sang, and had the love of the Lord in his heart, which caused him to always have a brilliant sparkle in his brown eyes. I know that he was the first grown-up to treat me as an adult.

Pastor Bob was different from any minister I had ever known. In fact, I have yet to meet another preacher who had the rapport with the young people that he had. He was always doing things for us. Even his interests were unlike any that your typical minister would exhibit. He bought an old Buick that required hours of meticulously dedicated restoration in an effort to return the classic to an original, mint condition. Bob and Lois came over to our house a lot for dinners, or visits. We spent hours together with their family. They joined us on many skiing trips. We went sledding together, bowling, pheasant hunting, and we all enjoyed many cultural trips to the zoo and the local museums.

Bob was truly a man of God—a man after God's own heart. His easy-going demeanor was a human reflection of the God who loves us. I remember that at almost every meeting, visit, or time of fellowship concluded with Bob blessing our time together with a heart-felt closing prayer. Our whole family was extremely close to both Bob and Lois, and considered them to be as close as family. In fact, when Lois gave birth to their first-born child, a girl named "Gina," Mom often talked about how they should make an arrangement to have Danny marry the girl when they became adults.

Pastor Bob took flying lessons after he came to our church. It wasn't long before he had completed his training for his private pilot's license. After several years of recreational flying, he felt comfortable enough to take a select few of our youth group on a short flight. There were about six of us who accompanied him on that excursion and together, we walked out to the tarmac where the rental plane was tethered. We watched with undistracted attention as Pastor Bob completed his pre-flight inspection of that shimmering aircraft. It was a meticulous inspection, one that all good pilots complete before even thinking about starting the engine to take flight. I was enthralled as we joined him in his inspection as we walked around that magnificent, shimmering piece of aerial precision. The white, riveted, aluminum skin that covered the plane glistened in the sunlight. My heart was beating so hard with the anticipation of flying, it was nearly pounding out of my chest. Reaching out to touch this mechanical wonder, my excitement continued to build in anticipation for my first-ever flight into the bounds of heaven. I could hardly wait to board that wind-bound beauty to soar through the clouds like an eagle in flight.

Since the plane was a low-winged Cherokee 150, Bob could only take two of us at a time. He would take-off, fly a small circle around the local town, fly back to the airport to perform a maneuver referred to as a "touch and go," and take a scenic flight around the town of Boulder before heading back to the airport to land. Bob would then taxi to the visitor's center, where the rest of us were not-so-patiently waiting for our turn. Tim and I got to go together on our flight, and as luck would have it, he got to ride in the front seat since he was about twenty pounds heavier than me. At first, I was extremely disappointed that I had to take a back seat for the dream-ride of my lifetime. Maybe that was partially attributed to my increasing paranoia about being a bit of a shrimp, since Tim's growth spurt had already taken hold, allowing him to grow to be several inches taller, along with a few pounds heavier than me. But, as soon as we started our taxi toward the end of the runway, I forgot all about where I was sitting.

I had dreamed of flying nearly all of my life. Growing up, I dreamed of becoming a pilot in the military, possibly flying helicopters or becoming a bush pilot missionary in a third-world country. Those magnificent flying machines fascinated me. I drooled whenever I got a chance to closely inspect any aircraft. As long as I could remember, I would have dreams about flying, of soaring through the sky unfettered by the bounds of gravity. Although, in my mind, it was always me flying across the treetops in control of the wind and air streams of the atmosphere. It was like Peter Pan in Neverland, my outstretched arms would be my sails as the wind lifted me from the confines of these earthly bounds of reality. I would ascend to realms of heavenly wonders where iridescent rays of light permeated the clouds while illuminating my visions of life. I never had a plane in my dreams. All I ever had to do was spread my arms to begin sailing across the confines of space and time. Dr. Sigmund Freud could probably share some insight into the meaning of those dreams, which could more than likely explain a few of the quirks that I have, along with the reasons I am the way I am!

Oh, how I loved to fly. The engine roars with a power that vibrates through your being, as it taxis down the runway while picking up enough speed to become airborne. To feel the plane shimmy and shake as we accelerated brought every nerve in my body to life. I still remember the butterflies fluttering out of control in my stomach when the front wheel lifted off the ground, and the plane rotated upward, causing the bright blue sky to be clearly exposed in the windshield. The force of the acceleration pushed me solidly back into my seat. Pastor Bob handled that plane like he had been flying all of his life. I remember him singing as he guided his craft through the sparse clouds, toward the deep-blue splendor of the Earth's atmosphere.

It was with dreaded anticipation that our flight too quickly came to an end as we made our final approach for landing, gently gliding over strobe lights highlighting the path toward the runway. Not only was I physically flying on that first plane ride, but I was emotionally in orbit. It took me weeks from my flight to re-enter the atmosphere and plant my soaring spirits on solid ground. Of all the things Pastor Bob did for us in that small youth group, (and they were too many to remember), that adventure was by far the most memorable.

I remember the night before camp as if it were yesterday. Tim had come over to my house to spend the night, since we had to be at church bright and early Monday morning. We went to bed fairly early, but the adrenaline was flowing too quickly to fall right to sleep. The anticipation of a trip away from home with no siblings or parents around to tell us what to do had us both on edge. We had never before been away from home on our own. Well at least, it seemed as if we were venturing out on our own. The thought of being old enough to go on a week-long adventure had us both on a natural high. We lay awake on the hot summer's night talking about all the fun life had to offer. We talked about the upcoming camp, about what to expect, what we could do, and of course, as teenage boys always do, we talked about the possibilities of meeting girls; lots of girls.

Even though we could never show it publicly at the time, especially in front of our families, we both had dreams of romantic strolls in the moonlit nights within the confines of the tall, bristling pine trees. Where the sweet smells of summer permeated the air, while the cool mountain breeze awakened your senses, making you more alive to life, dreams and love. We talked about what our "True Loves" would be like: rambling on about the color of their hair, to the sparkle in their eyes, and even the texture of their skin. We lost ourselves in the description of the perfect woman that was destined to come our way, going so far as to describe the softness of her voice, the beauty of her smile, and, most importantly, the sweetness of her soul. We were quickly emerging from boys, preparing to become men. The thought of what the future held kept our minds spinning through most of the night. Every time one of us would begin to nod off, the other would spout off with another profound insight to living. When morning finally arrived, both of us were almost too tired to really care about beginning the journey.

The drive out of Denver took about ninety minutes. Even though we left fairly early, by the time we arrived at Id-Ra-Ha-Je the sun was beating down in the cars and the mountain air had lost its chill. When we drove into the big circle drive at the edge of the meadow we could see crowds of campers scurrying about the grounds, unloading their suitcases and sleeping bags from their vehicles. The camp was alive with all kinds of teenagers, eagerly bidding their parents farewell. All the activity reminded me of an ant colony, alive with the congested chaos of work to be completed with too little time to accomplish the task. By the time we made it down the circle drive to the bustling activity of the main lodge, we were anxious to get out of the car to stretch our legs. We probably looked like a bunch of gangly, skinny-legged chickens emerging from the cars as we stretched our necks, while standing on our tip-toes to get the blood circulating once again. All the while, we were checking out the mix of campers to see if there were any familiar faces around, but, even more importantly, if there were any good-looking "ladies" arriving. By the time the last of the parents were driving away, we had all settled in for an exciting week of discovery.

It was amazing that as soon as we arrived, you could feel an exhilaration in the air as folks were scurrying about the cabins, cautiously choosing their bunk for the week's stay. As Tim and I made it into the main lodge, we saw a few familiar faces among the crowd; Pastor Anderson and his wife, along with his kids, were busy helping register kids, then pointing them to their respective cabin. He was the pastor of Grace Memorial church, but had served at our church on an interim basis before Pastor Bob came on board. Tim and I hurried to find our cabin as we scurried around the facility with a suitcase in one hand, a pillow under an arm, with our sleeping bags neatly tucked beneath the other somewhat free arm. The first thing we did when we finally found our accommodation, was to pick out our bunks. We each picked out a lower berth. Tim's was right across the room from mine, so we proceeded to roll out our sleeping bags and fluff our pillows before placing them at the end of the bunk, and then quickly made ourselves feel at home.

Before long, all the campers had settled in, and the bell tolled as an indication we were being summoned to the chapel for an opening service. I don't remember the theme of each camp, but I do remember that the organizers embraced the philosophy that the busier they kept the kids, the less trouble there would be during the week. Every minute of the day was occupied with all sorts of activities. Worship services, hiking, volleyball, softball, mountain climbing, water fights, competitions, talent shows, and the list goes on. There was a morning worship service every day with singing, usually accompanied by a guitar, skits, scripture readings, and mini-messages regarding the importance of developing a personal relationship with God. Each of the mini-messages brought spiritual relevancy to everyday life, including ways to apply that relevancy in a personal way.

After the morning service, we were offered the privilege to clean out the cabins, while also requiring us to tidy up the grounds in the front of each cabin. Each day, the staff would complete a white-glove inspection of the cabins to ensure that we didn't create too big of a mess, or get out of the habit of cleaning up after ourselves. Of course, the inspection provided a competition of sorts between each of the cabins, with an unspecified reward waiting for the winners at the end of the week. My favorite part of this morning ritual was coming up with a short memory verse to display in front of the cabin using small stones, twigs, branches, and pine cones. I still remember one of the scriptures we used, "For the Word of God is living and powerful and sharper than any two-edged sword" (Hebrews 4:12 KJV). Not to brag or anything, but our cabin always received extra kudos for our creative biblical application displayed proudly by the steps in the front of our quarters. However, we usually lost a lot of points for all the dust bunnies found under the bunks, but what could we say, we'd lost all of our dust bunny traps, and we weren't prepared to do windows either.

After cabin inspection, we were given quiet time to memorize a daily scripture verse. I always found it pretty easy to memorize things, even though my long-term memory had a tendency to forget where I'd placed those files. I could memorize things extremely quick, so after memorizing the verse, I would find Tim sitting out underneath a pine tree, or basking in the sun, perched on a giant boulder, where I could help him finish memorizing the assigned verse. After we finished with our assignment, we would go back to the things that boys do best, checking out the girls. Along with, trying to device a new scheme or two in an effort to impress a select few of the cutest ones.

Immediately following quiet time the serious activities began—GAMES! One of my least favorite games, however, involved pitting one person against another in a form of "jousting." There was a log fastened between two pine trees about three feet off the ground, with wood chips piled deep below this makeshift jousting horse. The log was just high enough off the ground that your feet wouldn't touch the ground. Needless to say, as a child, I didn't have too many fond memories of any type of horse, whether it was a swing-set horse, or the kind that neighs, snorts and attracts flies. So, the game had two people sitting face to face, about three-feet apart on this smooth, twelve-inch-diameter crossbeam. We were each given an old, feather-filled pillow and then given instructions that the object of the game was to see who could knock their opponent off the precarious perch by swinging the pillow like a knight on a mission to save the damsel in distress.

It was just my luck that Tim and I were paired off to fight one another to the proverbial "end." Did I mention that at that point in our adolescence Tim had several inches of height over me, along with an extra 20 pounds or so? Having an innate competitive spirit burning deep within my heart, I shrugged off the disadvantage, agreeing to give it the old "college try." Tim and I assumed our positions as the throngs cheered us on. I could hear the kids calling out the names of their hero of choice. As we tightened our grips on the corners of those old pillows, I'm sure that all the fair maidens were impressed with the rippling muscles of our forearms and biceps. With our jaws clenched in unrelenting determination, and our eyes sternly focused on the opposing challenger, we lowered our heads toward one another like two bull elk preparing for the rut. The cheers were reaching a deafening roar when the referee raised his hand to signal the start of the joust. I raised my pillow back behind my head, ready to deliver a fatal blow, when suddenly, Tim beat me to the punch. One swing of his mighty pillow and I was lying face down in a pile of wood chips, spitting splinters and sawdust out of my mouth.

The crowd drew silent as I lay motionless on the ground, trying to figure out my next move in an effort to recoup my beaten pride. It was obvious I hadn't impressed any of the fair maidens with my overpowering strength or stamina. "Maybe I could impress them with my superior sportsmanship?" I thought to myself as I pulled myself up to give Tim a congratulatory slap on the back. As I stood to my feet, the crowd once again cheered, knowing that I was none the worse for the wear. However, the whole time I was congratulating Tim, I was thinking ahead to the next challenge, thinking how I could impress the crowds with my agile tenacity, my leopard-like speed, or my astounding athletic ability. I knew one thing for sure, I had to quit accepting challenges that involved any type of brute strength.

The joust wasn't the most embarrassing part of church camp, though. That moment happened at the place called "the Fort." On the grounds of the camp was a full-size replica of a fort, you know, the kind that are made out of Lincoln logs, only this one was life-size. It came complete with watchtowers on each corner, along with a hinged gate big enough to drive a Conestoga wagon through. It was nestled in a peaceful meadow on the side of the mountain, encircled by magnificent pine trees that reached nearly one hundred feet into the mountain air. The mighty pines hid the fort from the view of any marauding hostiles. A flag gently fluttered in the breeze, just above the gates of this wilderness sanctuary. The flag was the Christian flag; white satin made up the body of the banner with a red cross emblazoned upon a field of blue, resting in the upper corner. It was a welcome symbol of hope for the weary travelers who sought refuge from the worldly dangers that are encountered along the trails of this mountain wilderness. It was a safe haven, more of a sanctuary from the storms that rock our world.

One afternoon we took a hike up the mile-long, rock-covered trail that wound through the tall pines leading to the fort. As we entered the gate, we were surprised to find an authentic chuck-wagon meal waiting for us. Tim and I had figured out this camp thing pretty well, and we each had an adoring young lass by our sides. It was a summer-time romance entwined with the reality of first-loves of which dreams were made of. Tim's friend was named Debbie. She was a perky, blue-eyed blonde that was almost as shy as he was. It's amazing that they ever got to know each other in the few short days that we had been at camp. My girl's name was Joyce who happened to be a preacher's daughter from the small town of Salida. She had medium-length, dishwater blonde hair, but what really attracted me to her were her radiant, emerald, green eyes. She had the prettiest green eyes that I had ever seen. Why, if you went by her eyes, you'd have thought she was of full-blooded Irish descent.

Joyce and Debbie had come over to our table at breakfast one morning. I remember that because I was so shy, I couldn't even ask them to pass the sugar to put on my thick, gooey oatmeal. You have to realize that camp food has the same reputation as school cafeteria chow. If you can imagine how awful plain oatmeal tastes without any sort of additional flavoring, then you can't help but to be sympathetic to my plight. As I sat there trying to force down that bowl of semi-warm, raisin-filled oatmeal with only one small glass of orange juice to flush it down, it was a near-torturous experience. But, from that morning's breakfast blossomed a week-long summertime romance that included starlit August nights, the exhilaration of holding hands for the first time (with a girl, no less), snuggling close around the bonfire and yes, of course, that first stolen kiss. Of course that was a monumental moment that sent this virile, young man's blood racing, and dispersed a migration of butterflies darting through the pits of my very nervous and rumbling stomach. It was the moment I had dreamed about for at least a couple of the last years of my young, girl-crazy life. You know, the kind that dreams are made of as you savor the softness, the gentleness, the sweetness, of your first love's luscious lips when they finally meet within the excitement of trembling anticipation.

Well, with our girls on our arms, Tim and I hiked up to the old fort like a couple of peacocks, proudly showing off our colors. Once we got inside the fort, we sat down to a meal fit for a college student. A college student on a limited income anyhow. Hot dogs, beans, coleslaw, and cherry Kool-Aid, all of which make up the finest of camping cuisines. After gorging ourselves on the traditional chuck-wagon delicacies, the camp staff decided it was time to once again work off some more of our youthful energy with another competitive challenge. They thought it would be a great idea to have some Indian leg-wrestling matches. Well, this time, I knew I was in luck. Tim and I had frequently engaged in a makeshift leg-wrestling challenge. I had a substantial lead in the win-loss column for this event. Knowing that I could beat Tim more times than he could beat me, I knew I could take on any of the other male campers who might be up to the challenge.

Even though it wasn't as important to impress all the girls with my athletic prowess, now that Joyce and I were friends, there was still that inner fire of masculine competitiveness just dying to show off for the world to see. So, I quickly jumped onto the damp, musty mat to lay down next to a kid named Steve. As the referee counted we each lifted up our leg in unison with each count. When the referee reached three, I raised my leg in a burst of energy and locked knees with Steve. Instantly, I rolled him over for the win, but in the process, a naturally occurring phenomenon exploded. Something that had never happened to me before, at least, in a public setting. The chemical reaction of too many beans mixed with the gastric juices of my digestive tract blew out of me with a thunderous blast. To my dismay, I think everybody in the camp heard it too. I couldn't believe it. I wanted to find a rock to crawl under as I had just passed gas in front of the entire church camp. Even worse was the fact that I had sent the entire camp running for cover, holding their noses, and I did it in front of a girl. It took a while to live that one down, and for the rest of the camp Steve used it as an excuse for his humiliating loss in the leg-wrestling match. After a couple of days the razzing finally dissipated. There was a great lesson to that embarrassing moment though; I learned that no matter what happens in life that "This too shall pass."

Camp really was like an Olympic event with all sorts of competitions. The best event that we ever experienced during camp was sort of an improvisational competition that erupted spontaneously. It all started one hot afternoon right after lunch when everyone was getting ready to go out to the softball field for yet another competitive activity. In Colorado, they have a saying about the weather, "If you don't like it (the weather), stick around for a few minutes, because it's bound to change." Well, that's exactly what happened on this beautiful summer day. The clouds began to roll in, the breeze picked up, the sky turned black with lightning flashing across the stormy horizon. The crash of thunder sent everyone running for shelter toward the main lodge. Within minutes there was a downpour of epic proportions. It was reminiscent of the stories about Noah when the heavens opened their flood gates, allowing the rain to come crashing down in buckets. Everyone rushed back to the cabins trying to run between the wind-propelled rain drops in an effort to find refuge beneath the patio of the main lodge. Did I mention that the main lodge happened to be the girls' cabin?

Truly, God must have heard our prayers, because we now had a legitimate excuse to hang out around the girls' quarters. We loitered around for what seemed like hours, making small talk with all the ladies, at least, the ones who dared to stay out on the porch too. We all waited anxiously for a sign that the rain would let up so we could get back to the fun of the structured activities. Well, as you can imagine, when you have sixty or seventy fully energized teenagers hanging around with nothing to do, especially since we were accustomed to having lots of structure in our days at camp up to that point, it didn't take us long to come up with our own source of structured entertainment. All it took was some wise guy with an empty Styrofoam cup to get things going.

Now, I don't want to mention any names here, but I just acted like I was going to throw a cup of water at an already rain-spotted counselor, and that was all it took. From that tiny little spontaneous prank erupted the most ruthless, out-of-control water fight the camp had ever witnessed. Before long it wasn't just cups of water, but buckets of water, shoes of water, baseball caps full of water and anything else that would hold water. The water was pouring out of the sky like Niagara Falls, filling the drain pipes with more water than they could hold, which caused the gutters to completely overflow. It was the counselors taking on the campers, and we outnumbered them by a ratio of 10-to-1. Pretty good odds, I might add, at least from our perspective. We were unmerciful, no one was spared. It was the worst water-fight massacre in the history of the county. The campers were triumphant, as well as squeaky clean. By the end of the day the score was Campers 1, Counselors 0. That is, until the next morning when we began our day with calisthenics.

Camp wasn't necessarily all fun and games, there were also some pretty serious moments of guided reflection and a vast amount of soul searching. At camp I learned the importance of reflecting on life, as I realized there was a need to look at your past, evaluate the present, and prepare for the future. Those distant trails along the path of life can guide us, affect our choices, and prepare our responses for challenges we face each day. The choices we make throughout life, along with the paths we decide to follow, need to be approached strategically, choosing wisely in order to avoid unnecessary pitfalls. More importantly, it was at camp that I realized my choices in life need to be made through prayerful consideration as I seek God's will for the direction I so desperately need.

The next morning after the water fight we were presented a message during a worship service. One of the pastors shared a relevant message about life. As a teenager, it's sometimes difficult to distinguish philosophical ramblings from concepts that are applicable and relevant. Add to that a tendency to hear one thing, then allowing your mind to wander to a thousand different things, makes it difficult to sit for an hour and get anything out of a message, at least for me with my hyperactive brain. I don't remember what the minister said on that particular day, but I do remember thinking back to the people in my life, at least to that point, who had made a difference. I thought about Mom and Dad, along with my Grandparents, especially Grandma and Grandpa Williams.

Of course, sitting still to listen to anybody talk for an extended amount of time was difficult for me at that age. I would have much rather been outside playing another game, or having another water fight. But as I sat there that day, trying to listen to what the minister was sharing, I started looking at my hands. My own hands reminded me of how my Grandpa's hands must have looked when he was my age. But, that made me think about how his hands looked at a much older age, right before he died. He had died just a few years earlier, and I still had emotional thoughts about him every day. Many times, just looking at my hands like I did that day, brought him instantly to my mind. That tiny little act had a way of bringing forth sweet memories. His death was my first experience with the final reality of mankind's destiny in this world. Even though he died at the age of 77 and he had lived a productive and satisfying life, his sudden death from a heart attack left the whole family in shock.

Grandpa Williams was a kind, caring man, who would have given the shirt off his back to anyone in need. Truly, he was the perfect grandpa, loving, playful, compassionate, and always there to spend some quality time with each of his grandkids. Thinking about his hands, I remember how his fingers were all twisted and bent from years of work as a carpenter, along with the many years of playing baseball. I can still see those old, leathery hands as he strategically took his next move on the checkerboard. He loved to play checkers with the grandkids, usually letting us win to help build our egos and competitive spirit. But occasionally he would let the old checker master come out to take the win from us when he only had a checker or two left on the board. After all, he had to keep us honest as he taught us one of the true realities of life, "You can't win all the time."

I remember how Grandpa used to get down on his knees, wrap those twisted, old fingers around the baseball to pitch to us, as all the grandkids would join in a makeshift game of ball out on the sprawling lawn on a summer's afternoon. Grandpa's hands were the rough, calloused hands of a working man, but his touch was always filled with love and concern. My Dad's hands were a lot like my Grandpa's hands, and I remember both of them, in spite of the condition of their hands, having a very gentle touch. I remember walking beside both Dad and Grandpa as a little child, hanging on to their weather-worn finger. Their hands seemed so big and strong to me as a young child. It took my whole hand just to hang on to one of their fingers. I remember Dad taking the back of his forefinger and wiping away a tear from my cheek as a child, whenever my little heart was broken. He would pick me up, then tell me to dry my eyes while giving me a big hug of reassurance. There is something special about a Father's love! Greater yet, is the love that our heavenly Father has for us, His little children.

When I remember the hands of the people who have touched my life in profound ways, I realize that their hands were often the instruments used to demonstrate their love, sharing devotion with their family. In those deep moments of reflection I would ponder the question, "What do those hands really represent?" Through the years, I've realized that they are a symbol of strength, courage, caring and compassion. Hands hold within their grasp the dreams for the future, the regrets of the past, along with the hopes for a brighter tomorrow. Our hands display the virtues of love that allow us to reach out to touch the ones who hold a special place in our lives.

The Bible tells us, "For there is no good tree which produces bad fruit; nor, on the other hand, a bad tree which produces good fruit. For each tree is known by its fruit" (Luke 6:43-45). As I look back on my life, I see much good fruit harvested by the hands of people who made a positive impact on me. As I was growing up, I saw the faith that was enveloped in those hands, I saw support, empathy, hope, and endless devotion in the hands of my parents and grandparents. I also found caring, guidance and discipline through the application of those hands to my life, which of course, sometimes happened to be applied to the reset button for my better judgment gland. I was fortunate, the hands of the people who raised me pointed me down the straight and narrow path. They exemplified—they helped develop—a foundation of faith, built upon the promise of Jesus Christ. What better foundation for a child to experience than one that is built on the principles and application of love?

Those were the kinds of messages they shared with us at camp, the kind that made me think; the kind that caused me to reflect on the big questions of life. Through camp, I began to look at people in a different way, and even more importantly, at life in a different way. Camp opened my eyes to see things from a new perspective, not just through my self-serving eyes, but through the eyes of others. I realized that one of the most important things in this life revolves around building relationships with others. I do remember at the end of that message, the minister closed with one question. "If you died today, what would you want your obituary to say?" I know that sounds like a morbid thought for a bunch of teenagers, but that one question served as the catalyst for my new perspective on life. From that point on, I began to look at life not from the beginning to the end, but the other way around. I wasn't necessarily concerned so much about how other people would remember me at the end of my life, but I became aware, and concerned about the possible things the Creator of life would say to me when I leave this world and stand before Him at His throne. I recently heard a song performed by Mark Lowry that pretty much sums up my philosophy on life. When I die, I want to go with "nothin' to prove, nothin' to lose, and nothin' to hide."

That one, significant message, along with the experience of the recent loss of my grandfather, was the beginning of my spiritual awakening. One that at first caused me to have more questions than answers. But that's what a spiritual journey is all about; it all begins by asking the tough questions in search for the Truth. Questions that start with the stark realities of life. The reality of life in this world is that it is finite, it has a beginning and it has an end. It's temporal, regardless of how prosperous, generous, or successful we are. We will all meet an untimely end. There really is more to life than what we physically see before us. Life is filled with an abundance of challenges, tempered with sporadic periods of sheer jubilation, interspersed with moments of happiness, seasoned with a few tears, and hopefully, mixed with the contentment that can only happen through intimate personal relationships with family and friends.

The most memorable moment of my camp experience happened on the very last night of that first year's adventure. We started out after dinner on a night-time hike that wound up on the side of the mountain overlooking the town of Bailey. The hike had almost everyone huffing and puffing from the lack of oxygen in that thin mountain air. The staff had started a gigantic bonfire that helped take the chill out of the cool, mountain air. As we made our way through the maze of pine trees, we found ourselves in a grass-covered clearing. The flames of the fire cast a dim illumination on the last few hundred yards of the winding trail. When we reached the fire, we all plopped down Indian style, just out of reach of the searing heat. We settled in on the trampled, damp grasses on that mountain meadow, trying to make sure we didn't crush any of the delicate wildflowers that were scattered throughout the meadow landscape.

The smell of burning pine permeated the air while the crackling fire mesmerized us as we stared into the dancing, brilliantly colored flames. The fire illuminated the large wooden cross, made out of giant pine logs, highlighting the significance of this symbolic monument of faith. Embers and ash floated past the silhouettes of moonlit trees, disappearing in the vastness of the star-filled sky. They seemed to be absorbed into the stars of the Milky Way, as they fluttered through the constellations, spiraling their way past the stars that make up Orion's translucent belt.

I think it was fitting that the constellation Orion was noticeably above us in the night sky. Orion, according to one translation is "He Who cometh forth as Light." This constellation, according to Dr. James Kennedy, a renowned American pastor and author, symbolizes Christ's triumphant and glorious return to Earth. Mentioned numerous times in the Old Testament, this constellation portrays the mighty hunter with a raised club in His right hand, and a slain lion in His left hand. Orion can be interpreted as Christ, while the slain lion is said to represent Satan. The stars above us that night actually revealed the story of God's plan of salvation. They glistened with the reality of mankind's redemption. Before the foundations of the world were in place, God meticulously placed His plan of salvation in the expanse of the heavens. I am encouraged to know that within that plan, He knew that during my lifetime, on that night, I would be amid a spiritual awakening, as I realized the love He had for me!

It was prophetic that the glistening stars above, as they immersed us in their light to guide us to redemption, also pointed to the dawn of Christ's ominous return. Maybe that's the reason I have always taken an interest in biblical prophecies. We are told that one day, Jesus will return to take His children home. No one knows the day, or the hour, but one day that time will arrive, and we better be ready. Through the constellations of the universe, God has given us a map, which is shared in the very first chapter in the book of Genesis: "Let them be for signs, and for seasons, and for days, and years." Man has twisted and contorted the message of the Zodiac to meet his needs and purposes. The true message, scribed in the celestial realms, declare the glory of God, for those who open their eyes to His wonder.

The immenseness of the universe became blatantly apparent as we sat there that evening, within the realm of God's creation. Sitting in front of that fire, mesmerized by the dancing flames, I reflected upon all that I had seen, heard, and experienced in that week of spiritual awakening. We sang the songs we had learned, one last time. They were melodic reminders of the walk we had just taken together, along with the bond that had developed between so many of us. Pastor Bob played his guitar as we all sang the Ralph Carmichael song from the 1960s "*He's Everything to Me.*"

As the last chords of the guitar faded into the night, faintly floating outward through the bows of the gently swaying pine trees, I realized that there was more to being a Christian than just believing Jesus had died on the cross for me. I had been raised in a Christian home, where church services, Bible studies, and daily prayer was an integral part of our lives. I was raised knowing that Jesus existed, that He willingly paid the price for my sin, and after dying on the cross, He rose from the grave. All of that was an accepted fact in my life; I never had a doubt about any of those things. But, I came to realize during that week of camp that God really was there to help me find the narrow way. That could only happen if I committed my life to Jesus. I knew at that moment that I wanted to serve Him all the days of my life.

While Tim and I sat there under the cloudless, star-filled heavens, with the fire crackling and the breeze rustling through the pine trees, I knew that there was a decision I had to make. I chose that night to become a follower of Jesus. He had sent me a message; one that was as clear to me as the one He had presented to the fishermen on the Sea of Galilee, "And He said to them, 'Follow Me, and I will make you fishers of men.' Immediately they left their nets and followed Him" (Matthew 4:19-20).

When the service closed that night in a word of prayer, I made a confession to God. I asked forgiveness for the sins of my young life. I prayed that He would take my life and use it in whatever way He deemed appropriate. I chose to follow after Jesus. Though Tim and I never talked about it at the time, as we sat there together, I had a sense that he was touched in the same profound way. While we prayed on the top of that mountain, with our heads bowed and our hearts looking toward the heavens, I could literally feel the presence of God, reaching out to draw me close. I knew that my life had been transformed at that very moment by the hand of God. I also knew that my life would never be the same again.

As I reflect back on those days, I am grateful that God had touched us in such intense ways at that little church camp in the woods. I am amazed how so many lives happened to intersect at that time and at that place. Which, of course, has everything to do with God's divine plan for all of our lives. I have often wondered what would have happened if Tim and his family hadn't started going to our church when we were kids. I truly believe that God brought Tim to our church for both of our benefit. I had always been rather lonely at church, with no real friends in my youth group. Sure, I knew most of the kids, but there was nothing special that we had in common. But, there was something missing until Tim came along. In him, I found someone who I could share my spiritual questions with, openly and honestly, and he could do the same. I found a friend to pal around with, who I could always depend on to be there. In Tim, I found a friendship that would last a lifetime. Together, we discovered that God is always there. Wherever we go, whatever we do, God is there, just a prayer away, watching over us, guiding us, loving on us—if we open our eyes to see. We are never alone. Even though we might be apart from the ones we love the most, we will always carry a special place in our hearts for them. I will carry to the grave, the memory, the essence of those days of my youth, locked within the deepest recesses of my soul.

Together, Tim and I shared an amazing spiritual experience at church camp. Individually, we both made a commitment to follow after Jesus, with all of our hearts, our minds, and our strength. It didn't matter how long or short our lives might be, we had decided to follow Jesus, placing all of our trust, our hopes, and our dreams into His capable hands. We had been given a path to follow. Everything that we had, now rested in the faith we had placed in our Lord, Jesus Christ.

The sun does rise, the sun does set, the moon shines bright at night;
God saw the "day" that He had made, and knew that it was right . . .
Church camp days and Bible days, to learn of Jesus love:
Blessed days, Holy days, faith cometh from above.
Fun-filled days, exciting days, days of high adventure;
Quiet days, thoughtful days, with visions of the future.
Romantic days, first love days, thrill to that gentle kiss;
Moonlight walks, sweetheart talks, memories are made of this.
Red-faced days of embarrassment, a trait among the youth,
Time to find a place to run, and hide the awful truth.
Days to heed God's message, convictions draweth nigh,
The Holy Ghost is speaking; turn not your face awry.
Days of choice, commitment days, which path in life to take;
Once faith takes root in your soul, you know which choice to make.
Christian days, faith-filled days, of devotion, worship, prayer,
Reaching out to others, God's Holy Word to share.
Caring Days, sharing days, when lives become entwined,
The joys of shared togetherness, two souls will tightly bind.
All these days together, make up the world of boys;
The sad day falls so quickly—Time to put away the toys . . .

—Clarice D. Cook

CHAPTER 6

The Setting Sun

As I pulled away from Uncle Don and Lea's house, I looked in my rear-view mirror to take one last look at Tim as he waved good-bye from the driveway. So much had happened in the last ten months that I was having a difficult time processing it all. It was difficult to separate the realities of what was happening with the hopes of wishing it was only a bad dream. My mind whirled with memories of the last thirty years as I gazed at the golden, glimmering hue of the setting sun as it slowly crept beyond the flat-top mountains behind Golden, Colorado. As the shadows began to creep into the cabin of my car, I felt all alone with the memories of the past, accompanied with the dim dark reality of what was surely waiting for us in the not-too-distant future. Yet, the lingering rays of light emanating from that glorious ball of fire in the sky seemed to engulf me with a sense of warmth and comfort as I traveled home on that warm August night.

It had become apparent over the last few months that a life on this Earth, a very special life, was quickly coming to an end. With the glow of the setting sun just barely visible over the top of the mountains, I felt a reassurance that brought a sense of peace. Even though life ends here on this small planet called "Earth," that doesn't mean we have no hope for tomorrow. The peace that I was feeling provided comfort to know that when we pass from this life, we will step into eternity with our Savior. The setting sun seemed like a message from beyond that there will be a tomorrow. Maybe not in this life as we know it, but through Jesus we will find comfort, peace, and new life. As I pulled up to a stop sign, I paused for a moment to partake of this beautiful gift God had sent to me. I knew that this day was probably the last adventure that Tim and I would share together on this Earth. The sun was setting on his life. His days were numbered, as are all lives, but I knew that God was still at work. I was reminded of the days of summer camp, of our commitment to follow Jesus. It had never really dawned on me before how important that one moment had been. As I drove on, my mind wandered back to the start of this last adventure together.

Only about ten months earlier this chapter began to unfold. It had been some time, fourteen years in fact, since those exhilarating, fun-filled days of our childhood. Even though the years had flown by, it seemed like just yesterday that we were teenagers, enjoying our adventures. Many things had happened since those bygone days of childhood. Even though the bond still remained firmly in place, circumstances, distance and the pressure of everyday life as an adult had prevented us from seeing one another or sharing in each other's life as we had once done. Even though both of us would have rather maintained an ongoing relationship.

Tim's mom and dad had divorced when we were about eighteen. Their divorce caused some major changes within all of our lives and we all felt the ripples of domestic tragedy as it filtered through the entire family. Both Dorothy and Don had since remarried. Dorothy became Mrs. Frank Cochran and Don had married Aunt Lea after the breakup of her and Al's marriage. Things had completely changed for our one-time, close-knit group, requiring major adjustments for all of us. It was during this time that I discovered the devastation and brokenness that accompanies divorce. When divorce happens, the impact and the rippling effects of devastation has a negative impact on all the friends and family.

Tim and I had both, long-since grown up into men and we went our separate ways out into the world to make our mark. I had finished high school, then went on to attend college in Rangely, Colorado on a baseball scholarship. After one year of college, I felt inclined to get married. I ended up marrying Kristi, who had been my high school sweetheart. After we were married, I received an apprenticeship at

Eagle Claw Fishing Tackle (the "fish factory" as I liked to say) as a machinist. I was often amazed at how I happened to land a job at one of the premier fishing tackle companies in the world. They had some of the best fishing equipment known to mankind; yet, I was probably the poorest excuse for a fisherman that this world has ever seen. After working at Eagle Claw for about four years, and after obtaining my Journeyman Machinist certificate, I was offered a position teaching at the same high school where I had graduated. Having the opportunity to teach precision machining, welding and applied physics at my high school alma mater was one of the best things that ever happened to me. I spent many years working full time, while going to school part-time at night and during the summers at Colorado State University in an attempt to finish my Bachelor's Degree. I love telling people that my four-year college degree was the longest eleven years of my life.

Before my wife Kristi and I divorced, we had two wonderful sons, Brian and Dennis. It wasn't too long after the divorce that Tim was diagnosed with cancer. The last years of my marriage were a horrendous experience. It had become obvious that nothing could get worked out, and all the things that a marriage was supposed to be just wasn't there for either of us. After years of struggle, we both finally agreed to go our separate ways, while doing everything we could to mitigate the impact on the kids. Many people commented through the years that they have never seen two people work things out so well for the kids. Maybe that was true, but I will be the first to admit that divorce is a devastating experience and regardless of how well things go for the kids, there will always be some scars that will have to be dealt with in their lives. It was a period of my life that required me to do something that went totally against the foundations of my deepest desires. I thought that I would never be divorced. I believed that the vows I had taken were for life. An overwhelming sense of failure tried to consume me, and I feared that I would be labeled a failure for the rest of my life. It took a long time for me to start believing in myself again. It took a lot of love and patience from my family and friends, too.

Meanwhile, Tim had ended his education in the eleventh grade when he decided to go to work in the molybdenum mine up at Empire, a small mining town in the mountains where Don worked. He had lived with his mom for awhile before his marriage to Sue. It was during this time of his life that he and our other cousin Rick had gotten pretty close. They worked together at the mine for a few years, which allowed them to spend quite a bit of time together. Tim knew from the moment he first saw Sue that she was the one he would eventually marry, knowing from the start they were destined to be together. He was crazy about her, and even though their marriage had some ups and downs, they managed to make things work.

Eventually, Tim and Sue moved down to the small farming community of Fort Morgan, where he was hired to work for the city. Fort Morgan was just a few miles from Snyder, where we spent a lot of time growing up. This quaint little town, which was the Morgan County seat, sat nestled along the South Platte River and was a great place to raise a family. Tim soon established a pretty comfortable life in this peaceful part of northeastern Colorado, and soon Sue and Tim had two sons together, Timmy and Chad. Life was at its fullest for Tim. It was a life that he had always dreamed about. He had a sparkle in his eye whenever he would talk about life in Fort Morgan. They had a home they dearly loved, since it had room to raise more than just a family. Their humble little acreage allowed them to raise sheep and pigs, as well as provide room for their horse and dogs. There was also plenty of room for Sue's garden where she planted all kinds of summer delicacies that, when harvested, were canned to be used throughout the fall, winter and spring to feed the family. Their home was surrounded by tall Elm trees which served as both a windbreak, a sunbreak, and a snow fence as the trees sheltered the house from the harshness of all the elements. It was a home for raising a family. Here in this small town on the eastern plains of Colorado, they had found their personal utopia. Ironically, it was here in Fort Morgan, the same county where his life began, that tragedy interrupted their lives.

Dorothy and her new husband Frank had just moved into a new house that they were in the process of fixing up. They were both pretty excited about the prospects of this new purchase, which was quite the fixer-upper. However, neither Dorothy nor Frank were capable of doing a lot of the necessary work themselves to make this place, well, let's just say, livable. Dad, who was capable of doing nearly anything around the house, volunteered to help them out. Well, actually, he might have been asked to help out, and knowing Dad, there was no way he could refuse helping out his sister. Anyway, he ended up going over there a lot to lend a carpenter's hand. Of course, Mom wasn't one to sit at home while Dad was helping out, so she was over there too, scrubbing, painting and decorating in an effort to get the place presentable. Really, it was a team effort, where a contingent of family and friends appeared to take care of the business of making this house a home.

The work had been going on for about a week when I decided to stop in on a Saturday to check out this family project. The house was literally abuzz with saws, vacuums, paint brushes, and scrubbing bubbles. Fresh paint permeated the air as the walls were being coated with acrylic splendor. Half the family was over there that day, with nearly all of them hard at work. I felt guilty for not being prepared to lend a hand. Tim and Sue were there with Timmy and five-month-old baby Chad. That was the first time I had seen Chad. It was amazing how the little guy at such a young age was the spitting image of his Grandpa Don. Although it was minus sixty years and counting.

Tim was out on the back porch working on a set of shelves that Dorothy had designed and engineered. Well, as far as they can be engineered without a drawing or a sketch, all she really had was a brief description of where she wanted them and how many. I stood around visiting with Tim as he went about his assignment with due diligence and determination to get it done before the day was out. He measured, cut, and assembled each piece with skillful craftsmanship. I'd hold a board, or hand him a tool as we continued on with our natural conversation. It didn't matter how long it had been since we had last seen one another, we'd pick up right where we'd let off. But, as we talked, I could tell that he wasn't feeling very well; it was obvious that he just wasn't his usual, jovial self. I didn't stick around too long that day since I hadn't come to jump in to help, but Tim and I had a nice visit talking about kids, families, jobs, and the chaos of life. I hadn't seen Tim since before my divorce so it was nice to have someone to share a few of the challenges I had encountered over that past year.

It was the next week that Mom called to tell me that Tim had gone to the doctor to try to figure out what was wrong. His ailments hadn't gone away, instead, they had continued to grow worse. The doctor he had been seeing in Fort Morgan provided two possible diagnoses. Since his work with the city had, on occasion, required him to work around the sewer lines, there was speculation that he might have been exposed to a form of hepatitis. The other possible diagnosis was he might have eaten some bad pork so he might have some sort of parasite attacking his liver. Not really knowing for sure what was going on with him, after weeks of tests, the doctor sent him to Denver to undergo even more tests.

I was out at Mom and Dad's one evening, and I was getting ready to leave when their phone rang. Dad went in to answer the phone as I waited patiently for him to come out before heading home. To my surprise, when Dad came out he said, "Aunt Dorothy's on the phone and she wants to talk to you!"

I was a bit surprised at first, but as I went inside, I had this feeling that it was bad news. She told me that Tim had been admitted to the hospital in Denver. She then added that they were pretty sure he had melanoma, a cancer that's generally associated with the skin, but can quickly spread to other organs. In Tim's case, it had spread to his liver. They weren't sure yet, since all of the test results weren't back. However, they were leaning toward some sort of diagnosis involving cancer. It wasn't hard to suspect though. Several of Uncle Don's brothers had died of melanoma, and Tim had already had a cancerous spot the size of a quarter removed from behind his ear that was diagnosed as melanoma when he was eighteen. In fact, after Tim's uncle had died from the disease almost ten years earlier he told his mom, "That's what I am going to die from."

As I pulled into the parking lot of the hospital, I paused for a moment to finish listening to a song that was on the radio. It was the song "I'd Rather Have Jesus," with music composed by George Beverly Shea, and lyrics written by Rhea Miller. I thought of the irony of hearing that song at that moment. The song that was leading me into this moment of time was the same song that the church camp was named after, Id-Ra-Ha-Je. The place where Tim and I had placed our lives into the loving arms of Jesus. The words of that song still echo through my mind. "I'd rather have Jesus than silver or gold. I'd rather be His than have riches untold; I'd rather have Jesus than houses or land, I'd rather be led, by His nail-pierced hand. Than to be the king of a vast domain, or be held in sin's dread sway. I'd rather have Jesus than anything, this world affords today."

The melody was ringing in my ears as the words touched the depths of my soul while I contemplated the message that had just been sent my way. How important, how significant this message was, right there, at that particular moment in time. Surely, God was with us! Tim and I had made a commitment to follow Jesus all the days of our lives almost twenty years earlier at that little church camp in the mountains. I knew at that very moment, that no matter what was about to happen, Jesus would still be in control of our lives, and our destiny.

I gathered my composure as I wiped the tears from my cheeks and eyes. I took several deep breaths as I readied myself to go up to Tim's hospital room. I didn't know what to expect. All I knew was that I had to be strong. I had to show my lifetime buddy that I was still there for him, and even though the pain of the situation was invading the very depths of my being, I knew I had to put it aside to find the strength necessary to maintain my composure. I knew that the only way that would happen, was if I leaned on the everlasting arms of Jesus. I picked up the cassette player that I had bought for him, along with a tape of my favorite inspirational songs and stuffed them in my pocket as I began the journey up to his room. The words, "I'd rather have Jesus," still echoed through my mind, bringing strength and comfort to my soul as the doors of the elevator closed and the elevator began to take me to my destination.

I never liked the hospital atmosphere, the way they smell, or the feelings that stir within me when I have to go visit someone. Maybe some people see them as a place of healing and comfort. But to me, they seem cold, sterile, and, in so many ways, impersonal. Maybe my feelings stem from the time Mom went into the hospital to have her fourth child. Instead of coming home with the realization of potential dreams and aspirations, she came home empty-handed with tears and remorse. Mom's trip to the hospital when I was thirteen years old had totally disrupted our lives. The stability of my loving family seemed to almost crumble during that time when grief paid us a visit. It took months after little baby Gordon Lee was buried before our lives slowly began to find a semblance of the peace and security that we had known before his death.

Our family, which was characterized by its closeness and compassion, was fractured by sorrow. Mom and Dad seemed to grow distant not only from each other, but also from us. They each struggled to deal with loss the best they could, in their own way, and also in their own time. But, it was hard for a thirteen-year-old to see them so quiet, so unnaturally forlorn. I missed the way our family had been, but most of all, I hated to see my parents cry as a result of inconsolable loss. It was a time of great sadness for our family, but it was also a time of tremendous spiritual growth.

Our dependence on Jesus became clearly obvious as we all turned to the only hope that this world had to offer. Part of our comfort came from a dream that Mom had a short time before the baby was born. It was a highly unusual dream; a dream that at the time of occurrence was hard to understand, but one that she couldn't forget. It was a dream that she kept to herself until after the still-born birth of the baby. Her dream was about her father who had passed away just a few months earlier. Grandpa Williams had become a Christian in the later years of his life, and when he died from a heart attack at the age of 77, we found comfort and peace in knowing that when he took his last breath on this Earth, he was welcomed home by his Savior, Jesus.

As Mom shared her dream with us, it was obvious that she cherished this dream, as it provided her with a sense of closeness and assurance to her loving father. She told us that it was one of the most vivid dreams she had ever had. In her dream, she was surrounded by close family members as they were all gathered together at the family home where Grandma Williams still lived. In the midst of the animated conversation of a family gathering, her father, (Grandpa) suddenly appeared. The room instantly became silent at the realization that Grandpa was there in the midst of the get-together. Everyone in the room seemed to fade into the background as Grandpa approached Mom in what seemed to be just the two of them in the room, alone together. They carried on a conversation; Mom said she could never recall its details. But then, Grandpa drew closer to his youngest daughter, taking her by the hands, while looking into her eyes with deep love and compassion. Then, he softly told her, "I will comfort you!" As soon as he spoke these words, a bell tinkled in the distance.

Grandpa softly responded, “I have to go back now!” With that, he disappeared from her dream.

Upon waking, Mom was deeply touched, and even slightly troubled by her dream. The dream had been so realistic, so resplendent with crystal clarity, forever etching it upon her memory. She was puzzled about what her father had said to her. She became concerned about his words, “I will comfort you!” She pondered those words for days as she tried to make sense of them, while also trying to convince herself that it was just a dream, created by an overactive brain affected by hormonal changes associated with the pregnancy. Several weeks passed before the heartbreaking death of her full-term, newborn baby boy. It was then that her father’s words took on an intense meaning.

But that wasn’t the only dream that seemed to come as a message of comfort from God. Grandma Cook shared a dream that she also had just days before the baby was stillborn. In her dream, she saw the baby fall into a pool of water. Grandpa Cook, who was still alive at the time, ran to the pool to pull the baby out. As he was standing there, cradling the baby in his arms, Grandpa Williams walked toward him, then gently reached out to take the baby to cradle him close to his breast. “I’ll take him now, and he’ll be fine!” Grandpa Williams said, as he turned to slowly walk out of the fog-satiated dream with little Gordon Lee cradled in his loving arms. Both of these dreams brought an amazing amount of comfort to the family. I could never begin to explain where these dreams originated, let alone explain the coincidental circumstance of how they came within just a few days of the tragedy of losing the baby. What I can say, is that we found a vast amount of comfort in these dreams’ messages, and as far as I’m concerned, they were a message from God, sent to provide comfort to a family that was crying out in faith for comfort and peace. The significance of the dreams were comforting as we realized that this precious little baby would never open his eyes to the sin of this world, but rather, he would rest in the gentle, loving arms of our heavenly Father.

We found still more comfort in the ritual of Christian burial as Grandpa Williams’ grave site was opened, and the baby’s little white casket was gently placed on the top of Grandpa’s larger bronze one. In death, the baby that had never known his grandpa in this world, found rest atop a loving grandpa's remains. Jesus promised us comfort. In John 14:18 KJV Jesus said, "I will not leave you comfortless; I will come to you." And, He did. Through the world of dreams our family was given a comfort beyond these earthly bounds. Through Jesus, our family, along with each of our broken hearts found healing. In the process we grew closer, and our faith in Jesus also grew. In spite of this, as I walked down that hospital corridor, on my way to visit Tim, those dreaded past feelings flooded my heart. With those long-forgotten memories refreshed in my mind, the sound of my footsteps echoed down the long, shadowy corridor.

When I walked around the nurse's station, drawing closer to Tim's room, I could hear him talking to somebody. I peeked in to see that a doctor was standing by Tim's bed, asking him a slew of questions. I didn't feel comfortable going in at that moment, so I decided to lean against the wall right outside the door. I must have stood there for almost twenty minutes pondering the stark reality of recent events. Through the rush of thoughts filtering through my mind, I couldn't make out the questions that Tim was answering. Finally, an attractive, female nurse walked by and encouraged me to go ahead and go into the room. I didn't hesitate for a second since I didn't want to give her the chance to change her mind. As I walked into the room, just inside the privacy curtain, I got my first glimpse of Tim since our visit almost a month earlier. I couldn't believe my eyes, and I tried to catch myself in an effort to hide my shock. I don't know whether it was noticeable to Tim or not, but I couldn't believe the look of the man lying before me in that hospital bed. I had always known that Tim and his dad, Don, looked a lot alike. But lying there that night, Tim looked like a sixty-year-old man in that bed. He looked more like Don than Tim. He couldn't be the same man I saw less than a month earlier. A month ago he looked strong, healthy, and full of life. This couldn't be Tim, there was no way this was the thirty-two-year-old man that I'd grown up with. His complexion was pale, almost a light gray. He looked completely exhausted, worn out. He looked downright old! In fact, there was the look on his face, even in his eyes, that cried out he was dying. Traces of death had already started to leave their unmistakable mark on him.

I walked up to Tim, reaching out to shake his hand as he lay in the bed with the covers neatly tucked around him from the waist down. "Are you a relative?" the doctor inquired.

"This is my cousin, Lanny," Tim replied, then added for my benefit, "This is one of my doctors."

With the formalities out of the way, the doctor continued questioning Tim about every aspect of his life. The interrogation continued for at least another thirty minutes as I sat there listening in as a passive observer. The only information I ever provided was when the doctor asked about Grandpa Cook's cause of death, along with the type of cancer that had taken him. "Well, he did die from complications of prostate cancer, but he also died at the age of ninety-four," I interjected.

Finally, the doctor seemed to be satisfied with all of the information he had gathered, so he graciously excused himself as he made his exit from the room. Tim and I finally had a chance to be alone to talk. "I brought you something to help pass the time while you're hanging out in here," I said as I handed Tim the cassette player and the tape. "I thought maybe you'd like some inspirational music to listen to," I added.

Tim graciously accepted the gift as I said, "These songs helped me through some pretty tough times in my life."

"Thanks! I can't wait to listen to them." Tim replied as he placed the electronics on the table beside the bed.

Our conversation picked up right where it left off just a few weeks earlier. In fact, as I sat there in deep conversation, I was reminded of the nights we shared on some of our skiing trips, or maybe even the night before we left for church camp. The chatter came free and easy, and for a moment, I think we both nearly forgot the challenges that were coming. We had been reminiscing for about thirty minutes when the nurse came to take Tim down for another round of invasive tests.

The severity of Tim's illness was blatantly obvious. It was nine o'clock at night and he had been scheduled for several hours of additional tests. "Well, I'll walk you to the elevator, Tim," I said as they were putting him into the wheelchair.

While waiting at the elevator, Tim looked up at the nurse in a bit of panic, exclaiming "I think I'm going to be sick!" With that, the nurse darted off to grab a bag.

I knew he wasn't going to be able to wait, so I found a pile of empty cardboard boxes sitting by a trash can, and quickly picked one up to hand to him. I was never one to be able to watch any one get sick, what with my weak stomach and all, but this time, all I could do was feel concerned for Tim. "Are you alright?" I asked as he wiped the remnants of vomit from his chin.

"Yeah, I'll be fine," he said, before adding, "I'm sorry!"

"No need to apologize, Tim, you just work on getting better!" I responded empathetically.

About that time, the nurse came back with a pan, reaching out to hand it to Tim. "I think you're just a little late," I told her as she took the box from Tim's lap, replacing it with the pan.

She grabbed the handles of the wheelchair with a jolt, pushing Tim inside the elevator, tipping him back as she quickly spun him around to face the open door. "I'll be talking to you soon!" I called out as the elevator door began to close and as I cocked my head to the side in order to catch one last glimpse of him. As I waited for the visitor's elevator, I reflected on the events of the past few hours. It was obvious to me that Tim's days on Earth were numbered and he wouldn't be long for this world. I had just seen him face-to-face, and the presence of death was already overshadowing him.

I took the elevator down to the main level, once again making my way down the long, dark hospital corridor. When I walked past the chapel, I glanced in the open doors. I continued walking for a few feet when an overwhelming sense came over me. I felt that the doors were opened for a reason. I turned around to stand for a moment at the Chapel's doorway. It was almost as if God planted this verse in my head, "I stand at the door and knock, if anyone hears My voice and opens the door, I will come in to him, and will dine with him, and he with Me" (Revelation 3:20). I knew that the doors had been open for a reason, just for me, so I slowly walked up to the altar rail to kneel down. With my hands folded, and my forearms resting on the rail, I bowed my head to pray. My prayers were laced with visions of my past, of everything that Tim and I had shared together. I prayed for healing. I prayed for guidance. I prayed for strength. I prayed for courage. I prayed for hope. But, as I continued to pray, I realized that Christ is our Strength. He is our Courage. Jesus is the Light, the great Physician, and He alone is our Hope! I ended my prayer with, "not my will, but yours be done!" I walked out of the hospital chapel into the chill of a late summer's night knowing that God was still in control, and I found peace in His solace.

It was just a few days later that Tim was told the diagnosis. Our fears had been confirmed. He had melanoma. He was told by his doctors that he had maybe two months to live. How do you react to news like that? As your mind swirls in an almost dream-like confusion, how do you react? What do you do? Where is your hope? Tim reached out to the only hope that is available to any of us, he reached out to hang on tight to the weather-worn wood at the foot of the cross. He pulled himself up to his knees and held on to the cross of Jesus with everything that he had within him. He wrapped his arms around the base of that tree, buried his face against it as he grasped the hope that the cross has to offer. Tim embraced the foundation of his faith. He clung to the old rugged cross as he fought for the strength to carry the burden that had been cast upon his shoulders.

His courage, along with his matter-of-fact attitude, mirrored his faith in the living God. His faith was profoundly evident as he began to plan for his last days. He signed a living will so that he wouldn't be resuscitated when he passed from this life. He began the preparations to get his house in order for the time that was fast approaching. He knew that with the short time he had remaining, there was just one message that had to be shared with his family, and with everyone he encountered. It was the Gospel Message, the message of God's love for us through the redemptive blood of Jesus Christ. I quickly discovered that instead of me being a source of strength for Tim, he was a source of hope and strength for all of us. He seemed almost anxious to begin this final journey. He knew he had just a short time left, and he knew that there was a lot of work to be done before he was gone.

The next day, when they began the chemotherapy, I decided to go back to the hospital to sit with him for a while. In my desk drawer at school I kept *The Christian Worker's* Edition of the New Testament and Psalms. I always had students scrounging around through my desk when I was out in the shop, and I always thought that maybe one of them might pick it up to get some good out of it. I picked up that New Testament and decided that I would give it to Tim so that he could read it while he was alone either at home or while he was in the hospital. On the inside of the pocket Bible, I inscribed a few encouraging words, words that would remind him how special he was and how much our friendship had meant to me.

As I entered the hospital that evening, I walked past the chapel, noticing that the doors were closed this time. As I continued down the corridor, it occurred to me that even though the doors were closed, Jesus' arms would always be wide open, ready to draw me close. When I made it to Tim's room, I discovered that he had been moved to the oncology ward. I quietly walked into his room, taking a seat in the chair next to his bed. Since he was undergoing a chemotherapy treatment, he was sedated and sleeping peacefully. They had him raised in an almost sitting position, with all sort of wires, tubes and contraptions hooked up to monitor the treatment. I watched his chest rise and fall with each breath as he lay there, unaware of anything going on around him. I didn't say a word as I sat there for an hour. I just sat there, reminiscing about all the things we had shared in this life; the good times, the playful times, and even some of the more difficult times. I pondered how his son Timmy had reacted to the tragic news of his dad's terminal illness. His initial reaction was anger toward his father. A normal reaction from any child thinking about a parent leaving them behind, no matter what the cause of the abandonment. To a child, I'm sure he felt like his dad was betraying him. I can't even imagine the emotions Timmy felt at the tender age of eleven as the security of his life was being destroyed. What would he do without a father to serve as a role model, a disciplinarian, and a guiding source of encouragement?

I thought of the important role that our fathers played in our development. What would we have been like without that modeling and guidance? Then I thought about baby Chad. "He's not even a year old," I thought as I realized he would never get the chance to know his dad. I knew that I couldn't let that happen. Somehow, I had to be able to share the adventuresome stories of his father. There were so many questions. There were so many fears that I had to overcome; yet, all I could think about was the dread of facing these realities head-on. But as I continued to think about the current reality, my greatest concern was for Tim and his family, including his mom, dad and sisters. They were the ones who would suffer the most. They were the ones who needed God's strength and comfort.

I didn't stay too long that night. With Tim sleeping so peacefully, there really wasn't much I could have done. To be honest, there really wasn't much that I could have been able to talk to him about at that point in time. Maybe it wasn't so much for him that I came to visit that night. Maybe it was really more for my own healing that I was there. I just needed to sit there, resting in the closeness of the best friend I had ever had in my life. When I got up to leave I placed the New Testament on the table by his bed, next to the cassette player that I had given him the night before. I knew that he would find it there, allowing him to know that I had been there to see him. When I walked out of the door of his hospital room, I turned around to take one last look at him lying in the bed. "See ya later," I whispered. "Take care of him Lord!" I prayed.

Tim was in the hospital for several more days after his initial treatments. After they sent him home, he was scheduled to go back every week for additional treatments. Regardless of the number of treatments, his prognosis remained the same. They had been honest with him though, as he knew his time was limited and that in the best case scenario, the treatments would possibly prolong his life for a short time, but that would be all he could expect. He was grateful for any additional time that the treatments might provide as he needed time to prepare his household and his family for the inevitable. He amazed me with his determination to make everything right as he took advantage of every precious moment he had left. During those days he lived each moment to its fullest.

When he got back home, the first thing he did was to find a church to start attending with his family. Both of us had drifted away from the church after our experiences with the small community church that we attended as kids. Neither of us had turned our back on following Jesus, but we had our fill of organized religion along with the politics that had engulfed the true mission of the church of our childhood. Besides the politics, the pastor that had replaced our beloved Pastor Bob insisted that God wasn't omniscient, omnipresent, or omnipotent. That viewpoint didn't set well with any of our family as we had personally experienced the true power and presence of the God that had seen us through the many challenges of life. Tim knew the importance of ensuring his family had a relationship with the same Jesus that he came to know at church camp. The remaining time he had left was devoted to that cause. He wanted to make sure that as baby Chad grew up, he too would have the opportunity to follow after the faith of his father. Within a few months of Tim's diagnosis, Sue and Timmy were baptized at the First Christian Church in Fort Morgan.

Tim went so far as to plan his own funeral service, even picking out his headstone and cemetery plot. Through all the challenges, he continued to live, and just as important, he continued to hope. As I had learned through all of those years of playing organized baseball, the game wasn't over until the final out is called. In fact, after several months Tim actually started eating fairly well, putting on a bit of weight. He had dwindled down to less than 140 pounds from his original weight of close to 200 pounds. It was encouraging to see his positive attitude as he continued to enjoy life even when things seemed hopeless and out-of-control to most of the family. Everywhere he went, he would tell people about the love of Jesus, encouraging them to find hope in Him alone. It didn't matter whether it was a distant relative, or a close relative, or even another cancer patient in the hospital, he would share his testimony of what Jesus had done in his life. It was amazing how someone with only a short time to live, and whose life on Earth was obviously quickly coming to an end, could be so full of hope. He continuously talked about how he would be healed. Not necessarily in the way we were hoping for, but in the eternal sense, according to God's promise. The first few times he told me that, I would respond, "I hope so," or else I would say, "That's what I'm praying for." But after a while, it dawned on me what he was really talking about. In not too long, Jesus would take this burden away, making him whole in the perfect sense.

In the passing months, Tim and I had the opportunity to spend a lot of time together. We probably visited each other more in those few short months than we had in the previous fourteen years. We talked with each other on the phone almost every time he was in

Denver for another treatment. Often, I would stop in at his house in Fort Morgan whenever I was down that way on a trip to see my Grandma Williams. We talked, we shared—we even reminisced with each other trying to make up for the lost time that had separated us after growing up and getting busy with life. We even healed some old wounds that happen when friendships go their separate ways. In many ways, Tim was right about being healed. It was obvious that there was a lot of healing happening within our family. God was gracious to all of us during that time. Tim was looking better, and even feeling better. He was getting his strength back as he continued to work up a pretty healthy appetite.

Our prayers for Tim to make it to Christmas were answered. His health seemed to return in an amazing way. I remember Christmas dinner at Aunt Dorothy's that year. I don't think that I had been over to her house for a holiday dinner since I was a teenager. Tim and I were sitting together again, just like it had been twenty years earlier, except that his wife Sue and little Timmy were there on the other side of him. It was a time that memories are made of, as I was able to share that dinner with a very special part of my family. It hadn't been but a few months since my divorce was final, and I wasn't accustomed to being alone on a holiday without my two sons. The heartache I endured during this special season was nearly unbearable as I faced the holiday knowing that I would not be able to provide my sons with the traditional family like the one I was blessed to know as a child. The Christmas tree, along with all the decorations and lights that lit up the house, were nothing more than a façade. The reality of the season was that my heart was drenched with sadness as I tried to make a memorable Christmas for my boys. But with most of the people that were dear to me gathered around this Christmas table, it was impossible to succumb to the desperate loneliness that had accompanied me for the past several holiday celebrations.

Tragedy and crisis, such as the one we faced, helps to provide a new perspective on what is really important in life. It helps to re-evaluate the true blessings that God places in your life. As we joined hands to pray, I silently thanked the Lord for his bountiful blessings, for the family that He had given me: my sons, my parents, brothers, aunts, uncles, and cousins. I was blessed to be surrounded by family whom

I loved dearly. I was blessed to share one last Christmas dinner, along with a special day, with Tim.

The frosty cold of winter slowly turned into spring as the budding leaves and blooming flowers burst forth with new life. Tim was still alive, and doing very well. The hectic life at school that always hit this time of year didn't allow me to see Tim or talk with him as much as I would have liked. However, we did maintain contact with each other, and he was constantly in my prayers. Once spring turned to summer, which, of course, ushered in summer break, I knew I would be able to spend more time with Tim. I was able to stop in to see him several times during the summer, usually on my way home from seeing my brother Randy and Grandma Williams in Snyder. The last time I stopped in to say hi, I discovered that Chad had come down with a case of the chicken pox and Tim had gone to Golden to stay with his dad. As soon as I got home that night, I called him up on the phone. During our conversation, we decided to take a drive together the next day in order to have a day away. He was sure he was up to the task, so we confirmed the plans to venture out for a day of fun.

The next morning, I got the boys ready before heading out to pick up Tim at Don's house. We really had no idea where we were headed, or what we were going to do, but that was always the way we began our adventures together as kids. So as we climbed into the car and buckled up, I suggested that we head up to a small, tourist adventure called "Heritage Square." Tim agreed, and so we headed up the highway toward the foothills of the Rocky Mountains! This tourist village was a replica of an eighteenth-century town that was full of small gift and food shops. It had an old-time wedding chapel, a turn-of-the-century train that chugged around the perimeter of the park, race cars, bumper cars, paddle boats and a putt-putt golf course. There were all kinds of fun things to do and see. I knew that not only would Tim and I enjoy ourselves, but I also knew it would be a treat for Brian and Dennis.

When we arrived at the park, we decided to wander around a bit to check the place out. I always enjoyed the glass blowers in the little shop where the artisans were busy making all sorts of intricate sculptures. We discovered a rock shop which, of course, reminded us of all the rocks we use to buy to cut up in Tim's basement with his diamond blade rock saw. There were geodes, thunder-eggs fossilized fish, amethyst, rose quartz, along with Apache tear drops, moon stones, tiger eye, jade and turquoise. The memories came rushing back from our teenage years. Years spent cutting and polishing exquisite rocks that we would turn into splendid pieces of jewelry as gifts for family and friends. I'm pretty sure that most of the family was quite relieved when we finally passed through that stage of our youth. We made so many pieces of jewelry that we had a hard time even giving the stuff away. I still come across a few pieces of the stuff once in a while when I'm cleaning out a drawer or old box of memories. Of course, I never understood why our jewelry-making days were so misunderstood and underappreciated, but then again, I think that all teenagers are pretty much taken for "granite."

We took a stroll through the old-time photo parlor, checking out the myriad vintage costumes from a bygone era. We spent a few minutes talking about how much fun that would be, to dress up to get our picture taken the old-fashioned way. By this time, Dennis and Brian were getting just a little bit antsy, so we decided it was time to take a ride on the vintage, coal-powered, steam engine locomotive. We bought our tickets, presented them to the conductor, as the kids scurried aboard in unbridled excitement. The kids hurried ahead of us to pick out four seats as far forward as they could find. In fact, they were right behind the engine. We only had to wait a few minutes before the conductor cried out, "All aboard." Then the engineer gave the steam whistle a few blasts to let the town know we were pulling out of the station. The train chugged and jerked as we began our sluggish ride around the scenic railway of that western village.

Riding on that train brought my imagination to life as I saw images of what life must have been like in the days of our great-grandparents. The smoke from the engine billowed out of the tall, dark smokestack on the front of this steam-powered, mechanical marvel. The smoke, intermixed with particulates of soot and ash, caused our eyes to water, as the pungent smell of the burning coal irritated the sinuses. We gently rocked back and forth with the rhythmic swaying of the rail cars as we journeyed into a distant era. The clickety-clack of the steel wheels crossing the joints of the track echoed throughout the valley as the mountain breeze whipped through our messy hair.

Those types of experiences always took me back into another age. The kind that our forefathers knew. They always made me wonder how much different life must have been in the previous century. During those times, I always felt a sense of mortality, knowing that those who had lived before me had already passed through this world. The generations that had gone before me probably had the same basic hopes, fears and dreams for their lives that I have for my own. I often wondered if my forefathers had attained those that were important to them. I really have no doubt however, that most of them realized the realities of their fears before they took that final express out of this life. I was brought back from my mental wanderings by the haunting solace of the train whistle as we neared the end of our ride. How lonely. How eerie that long whistle blast sounded as it echoed throughout the mountain valley. It was a signal to the station master that the train was homeward bound. How prophetic? That haunting steam whistle was a signal—Tim was nearly home.

After the train ride, the kids decided it was time to ride the go-carts. I had always wanted to try my hand at driving those motorized, pint-sized cars as a kid. But the times we would go to the local amusement park, I was always too short to ride them. By the time I was tall enough, I had lost interest in speeding around in a kiddie-car, even if it was motorized. These carts were the miniature version, designed specifically for kids under twelve. So off they went to experience the joys of driving on their own. Fortunately, Brian and Dennis were the only two kids on the track, so I could forget my paranoia for a bit to sit back and relax. Tim and I found a spot beneath an old elm tree where we took a seat on a picnic table that was just next to the track. We enjoyed the shaded shelter that the tree offered as we continued on with our constant chatter. It reminded me of those long-forgotten years when the two of us would sit for hours, sharing thoughts, insights, and profound wisdom. As we sat there in total contentment, we decided that it would be a great idea to go back over to the photo parlor to have our picture taken. We had never done that together, so we decided there was no better time than the present to make a lasting memory. Besides that, it would make a great keepsake to give to our moms.

When the kids were finished with their rides, at least I was finished buying stock in the corporate exploitation that ran the excursion, so we headed over to the old-fashioned photo shop. Tim threw on a long, denim range coat as he mulled over the hat possibilities. He then proceeded over to the gun section to pick out his favorite weapon. He noticed a Winchester rifle leaning against the wall, and since it looked like the BB gun of his youth, he grabbed onto it, knowing that real cowboys always carried a rifle. He grabbed it by the small of the stock, and tipped the barrel against his shoulder before heading over to the bar to assume his photogenic position.

I picked out a long, white range coat, throwing it on as I rummaged through the pile of old hats. I was looking for one that displayed the true essence of the American cowhand. I found one that looked as if Little Joe had tossed it to the side so I plopped it on my head to take a look in the mirror for final approval. Then, I proceeded to check out the weapon closet, looking for the perfect accessory to complete my western fashion statement. I noticed a Colt 45 adorned with a leather holster and hand-tooled, leather gun belt, hanging on the wall. I slapped it around my waist, before picking up an old, double-barreled shotgun as I headed over to the bar. We both looked as if we had just stepped out of an episode of *Gunsmoke*. In fact, I couldn't help but glance around the room to see if Matt, Festus or Miss Kitty had made their way to the Long Branch Saloon. Actually, the only accessory that we were really missing were a couple of young, attractive dance hall girls hanging over our shoulders. We both knew, however, that photographic evidence like that could convict an old cowpoke of one of those Deadly Sins we learned about as children. Especially for Tim, since he was a happily married man.

We leaned against the oak bar, proudly displayed our firearms for the contingent to see, and then put on a poker-face. The kind of face that every gunslinger, and every gambler, this side of the Mississippi would envy. There had always been a bit of drama-king in each of us, so it was natural to play the part of a couple of wiry, old cow pokes. After the photographer snapped the picture, causing the flash to pop with a controlled flare, we horsed around a bit before taking our costumes off and returning to the twentieth century. After the picture was developed, we both decided to purchase a nice, eight-by-ten-inch glossy to commemorate our day together. What amazed me most about the sepia-tone picture was the way that Tim looked in it. The chemo-treatments, or else the cancer itself, I'm not sure which, had turned his skin color to a dark gray. He also had developed some half-dollar size moles that were almost pitch black on his neck, his forehead, and throughout his hair. But, in the photograph, he was the picture of good health. Why, he looked as healthy as a young stallion. Even though it was a sepia-toned picture, his color looked normal and there wasn't one blemish showing on his exposed skin. There was a great significance in that picture. Not only is it the way I'll always picture Tim in my mind, but I believe it was a divine reminder that through Jesus all things are made new. Tim would find the healing he continued to proclaim.

When we left the photo studio, we grabbed some snacks, along with something to drink, before deciding to head further up the mountain. I felt like there was one more place we had to visit before our day came to a close, at least the part of it that we enjoyed in the mountains. I had visited this place once before. It was a tranquil place of reverence. I knew it was a place both of us needed to share together as it was a place that would allow us to draw into the presence of God, in our own personal ways. The place is called Mother Cabrini Shrine, and it is located in the foothills, strategically perched atop a rolling hill that overlooks Denver and the entire eastern prairie of Colorado. There is a statue that stands at the top of the hill, facing east with outstretched arms welcoming the world to the entrance of the majestic Rockies. It's a statue of Jesus that stands probably twenty-feet tall. It is an ominous portrayal of Christ that draws your attention as you drive down the highway into Denver. Legend has it that Mother Cabrini, a Catholic Nun, had seen a vision on that spot sometime in the early 1900s. At the time, she designed a heart made of rocks on the grassy knoll as a memorial to the message she had received from Jesus. The statue was built quite a few years later, enduring the elements on top of the rugged hill. After the statue was erected, they also added a flagstone pathway that winds up the hill to provide easier access to the monument.

I couldn't believe how many steps led to the shrine. There must have been hundreds, maybe even a thousand steps that scaled the steep embankments making their way to the top. It was such a strenuous climb that flagstone benches were installed along the way to provide a place to rest so that a person's heart could slow down, and their lungs could catch a breath. I didn't know if Tim would have the strength to make it to the top, but he assured me that he would only go as far as he could, and then wait for us at that spot to come back down. With that decided, we began a long, winding ascent up the stone steps. About a third of the way up, Tim decided he would sit and wait for us. From the bench he sat upon, he had a good view of the statue, along with a great view of all the beautiful flowers and shrubs that lined the path. He knew his limits as he determined this was as far as he wanted to go. As Tim settled in on the bench, Brian and Dennis scurried ahead of me up the steps. When we finally made it to the top, I was awestruck by the enormity of the statue, as I tried to catch my breath. I wondered though, how much the statue would pale in comparison to Jesus himself if he was standing there in front of us. We didn't stay up there too long since Tim was waiting for our return. I stayed long enough, however, to say another prayer for my dear friend. Before we headed back down, I paused for a moment as I marveled at the great expanse that reached out to the horizon from this representation of Jesus—the great expanse where we had grown up—the eastern plains.

After spending time at the Mother Cabrini Shrine, I realized that Tim had never seen my new house, so I convinced him to come over with me until the kid's mom picked them up for their scheduled stay at her house. I assured him that afterward, I would take him back to Don's house before it got too late. Our conversation was non-stop. I don't remember everything we discussed, but the chatter flowed freely for the whole drive. After the kids were picked up by their mom, we decided it was time to get a bite to eat to curb the savage beasts growling deep within our bellies.

Before heading back to Golden to take Tim back to his dad's house, Tim suggested stopping by to see my younger brother Danny. They hadn't seen each other for years, and since Danny was always asking about Tim, I knew they would both enjoy a visit. Even though Danny was about six years younger than us, as we grew up, he would often tag along on our adventures. Danny and I always shared a closeness that most brothers never have. In fact, I was lucky to share a bond with my brothers that was surprising to most people. It's not a common thing that brothers could get along so well. Since Tim was like a brother, it was like we were all one big, happy family, and what was so unusual about it was that we all got along extremely well anytime we were together.

After our visit with Danny, we headed out to take Tim back to Don's house in Golden. Our conversation turned to the reasons we continued to believe in God throughout our life. Evidence of God's existence came from the many experiences each of us had that opened our eyes to God's wonders, and His presence. Many happenings were nothing short of miraculous. Even the so-called coincidences in life pointed to a loving God who was guiding us through a daily walk. The birth of a child, the dawning of a new day, a bird in flight, the wind whispering through the trees, the first snow of the season, the morning dew on a summer's garden, a flower in bloom, and the sun glistening off a mountain stream all provide evidence of a Creator who designed this wonder of a planet. As a Christian, I realized early in life that anywhere I looked, I could see the miraculous hand of God in the miniscule details of this Earth. Of course, to someone who doesn't believe in God, all of these things just happened to burst forth as a single cell split into the infinite intricacy of life itself. Personally, when I look at the amazing intricacy of this world, I can't help but believe someone had to put it all together. I don't have the faith to believe life just spontaneously exploded, creating the millions and billions of different cells contained in the world's expanse of living organisms and creatures.

We discussed the dreams that had come to both of our families through the years, and how those poignant dreams were often a source of hope and encouragement. Not only did we talk about the dreams that mom and Grandma Cook had regarding the baby, but I also shared with Tim a dream that my Grandma Williams had often shared. I had two cousins, nephews of my Grandpa Williams who were killed in Vietnam on the same day. During the weeks preceding their deaths, Grandma had a dream that caused her to believe they would soon be leaving this world. When Uncle Dick, who was Virgil's dad, came to the door one afternoon with tears in his eyes, Grandma already knew what had happened as she had seen it in a dream.

Another story I shared with Tim that day involved my own son Brian. When he was about five years old, we noticed a large growth on the back of his right knee. We immediately made an appointment for him to see the doctor. After being sent to several specialists, we were finally assured that his condition was caused by a leak in the bursa sac around his knee joint. It was similar to a ganglion cyst that many people get around their joints. A few months later, he somehow developed a swollen, very tender spot around his wrist. Once again, we took him to a specialist at Children's Hospital Denver who completed an examination. After the exam, I overheard the doctor discussing the case with two other specialists. I heard them say that he suspected Brian could have some form of lymphoma. I remember immediately praying for God's intervention.

The doctors scheduled several additional tests over the next couple of days, so the intense wait began. After getting as many answers as possible to my multitude of questions, I called my folks to let them know what was going on. As soon as we got off the phone, Mom walked out to the back deck. She leaned against the wooden railing to begin to pray. As she raised her head, opening her eyes, she instantly knew that God was listening. She knew with uncertain confidence that Brian was going to be fine, because off the deck, at a time in late July when iris never bloom in Colorado, was the most beautiful iris blooming with magnificent splendor. As it turned out, after another round of tests, the inflammation was caused by a bruise, not any disease. Brian was fine!

Maybe I was hogging the conversation most of the way back to Don's house, but I shared with Tim one last experience that provided proof to me personally that God loved me, and constantly kept watch over my family. I told him about one of my favorite experiences of all time. It was the blizzard of 1982, which hit on the morning of December 24. It was actually the event that allowed me an opportunity to meet my guardian angel face to face. Now, I've had a lot of people tell me that I'm nuts, but that's okay. I was there and I know what really transpired that afternoon as we were headed out to Mom and Dad's house for a Christmas celebration.

Mom and Dad had just moved into a beautiful, tri-level home that we had custom built for them on a two-acre lot. The acreage was about eight miles outside the city limits in a new subdivision. Not only was it a custom home, but it was one that Dad had designed, having a friend draw up the prints. It really was the home of their dreams. It normally took us about fifteen minutes to get to their house from our home in the city. Our Christmas Eve celebrations usually began around three in the afternoon, so when we woke up on that cold, snowy morning, we didn't feel any sense of urgency to rush around to leave. But, not too long after breakfast, the snowflakes started getting bigger as the snow quickly began to pile up on the streets and sidewalks. I decided it would be a good idea to pack the car with all of the gifts and food so that we could head out a little earlier than planned. As Kristi got the kids ready, I decided to go ahead and put the tire chains on our little brown Toyota Corolla, as an additional precaution. The snow was already about a foot deep when I finished chaining up the car. I finished packing the trunk of the car, and for no particular reason, I decided to throw in a couple of sleeping bags, even though there really wasn't any room to spare.

As we started out the back road that we normally took and with the kids warmly buckled in the back seat, it quickly became obvious that the snowplows hadn't cleared the two-lane highway at all that day. Not wanting to push our luck, we headed out to the four-lane highway, winding along the outskirts of the city, in an effort to get back on track. As we trudged along at about fifteen miles an hour, we passed a half-a-dozen vehicles that had slid off the side of the road and were unable to get unstuck from within the clutches of the deep, wet snow drifts. At one point, I was tempted to turn around to head back home, but once we made it to the highway, the sky began to lighten. With the snow letting up, we decided to continue on our journey.

Continuing to travel down the highway, the snow-packed roadway looked more like a war zone with abandoned vehicles littering the way. Cars, trucks, even tractor-trailers had slid off the road, becoming entrenched in the snow-covered ditches. We were at a point that we should have turned around, but there wasn't any place that would allow us to cross the median to head back. Besides, we really were only minutes from reaching our intended destination. Surely, we could make it a few more miles without any trouble.

Before we turned down 114th Avenue to make the last mile and a half of our journey, the wind picked up, causing the freezing snow to pile up into huge drifts that crossed the already snow-packed roads. There was a two-foot drift across the road making it impassable. It was obvious that we would have to turn around in an attempt to get back on the highway. With any luck, we could reach the next cross road, which was 120th Avenue. When we finally found our way to 120th, the storm had turned into a full-fledged blizzard with near-white-out conditions. Visibility was maybe twenty- to thirty feet, while the wind-chill had brought the temperatures down to well below freezing. The windshield, as well as the windows of the car, were almost completely fogged over. I had to roll the driver's window down to stick my head out into the elements in order to see where I was driving. Our trip, which normally took about fifteen minutes, was already into the second hour of driving. We were still more than a mile away from the folks' house. I knew that they would be worried sick since Kristi had called them right before we left home. We decided it was time to stop at one of the few houses along the road to try and call.

I pulled into a snow-drifted driveway as far as I dared before getting out of the car. I left the engine running with the heater blasting so that Kristi and the kids could stay warm, thinking hopefully that it might help the windows defrost while sitting there. I trudged through the knee-deep drifts of snow as I made my way to the porch that covered the step. The porch offered a bit of protection from the freezing wind that pelted my face with the harsh blowing snow. I stomped the snow off my boots, while brushing the snow off my pants, as I waited for an answer to my ringing the doorbell. I must have rang the doorbell at least four times, with no reply. Obviously, nobody was home.

My heart sank in near hopelessness as I turned to head back to the car. The gigantic, freezing flakes stuck to my face, and flew into my squinting eyes as I rushed back to the car with my head hunched down deep into my shoulders. "Nobody is home!" I barked as I slid back into the driver's seat which was wet from the snow that had blown into the car and then melted.

"What are we going to do?" Kristi desperately inquired with a tinge of despair dangling from her words.

"I guess we'll see if we can make it somehow!" I replied in an attempt to hide my fear. I wasn't to the point of panic yet, but I was extremely concerned about the circumstance we found ourselves in. The one thing I knew for sure is that we couldn't turn around to head back home.

As we pulled onto 120th Avenue, snow began to fall even harder. As we headed east, the visibility dropped to just a few feet beyond the front of the car. Once again, I rolled down the window to begin searching for the cross street we needed to take south. As we crept along at a turtle's pace, I strained to find a trace of the road as the blowing snow literally blinded me with its freezing force. The snowplows had been down the road we were currently on, which of course, piled the snow up almost to the top of our little compact car. It was like driving down a one-way tunnel. I couldn't see anything. There was nothing ahead of us but white. Everywhere I looked it seemed as if I was covered in a white linen sheet. I kept hanging my head out the window in an attempt to keep from running into the walls of snow on each side of us, built up by the snowplows. Suddenly, as we emerged from this tunnel of white, I discovered that we had reached the top of the hill. As my mind whirled in a frantic effort to determine our exact location, I realized that we had driven right past the road we needed to turn down. I quickly found a spot in the road that allowed us to turn that little Toyota around so we could head back once again in the same direction from which we had just come. This time I drove even slower, stopping every few minutes to verify our location in relation to the road we were frantically searching for.

At this point, I was extremely concerned about getting stranded with a six-month old and a two-year old in the back seat. Visions of a Christmas Eve tragedy began to infiltrate my thoughts as I began to ponder the ramifications of my foolishness, wandering out into a blizzard. I knew we should have stayed home where it was safe. I let my pride interfere with common sense as we set out that day in weather that warranted staying put. I kept thinking about what would happen if we were stranded in that powerful storm. We could freeze to death on the most sacred of holidays. How would that impact my family? How would they be able to cope with such a tragedy? My mind whirled with the prospects of a multitude of disastrous endings to our seemingly hopeless plight. Suddenly, I was brought to my senses from my dreaded thoughts as I caught a glimpse of the street sign that we had been searching for so diligently. Maybe, our luck had finally changed, and we could finally reach our destination.

I turned south on the street and traveled several hundred yards before coming to an abrupt stop. Right in front of us stood a three-foot-deep snow drift. It completely covered the road. We sat there for a few minutes in total silence. The sound of the car engine, along with the whirling sound of the heater masked the rushing sounds of the wind-whipped snow outside the car. I dropped my head to the steering wheel, resting my forehead on my hands as I contemplated our next move. The snow dripped off my stocking cap as it melted from the heat of the defrosters, saturating a spot on my jeans with its cold reality. I sat there for several minutes, searching for an answer, realizing that this situation was completely out of my control. I had no idea how to get my family to safety, out of reach of this deadly storm. As I sat there shaking like a leaf in the wind from the cold that had permeated my entire body because of my dripping-wet clothes, I began to pray. At first I prayed silently. But before long, as I turned the car around in an effort to try to make it down 120th Avenue to where my friend Jerry's mom lived, my prayers turned into spoken pleas of desperation to God. Actually, it was probably more like a mumble, but my prayer was that we could make it back down 120th to Flo and Ron's house. Even if they weren't home, I knew they would forgive me if I broke into their house to find refuge from the storm.

As we began to retrace our path back to 120th, with my head once again hanging out the window trying to keep an eye on the road, I continued to pray out loud. Kristi kept looking at me and asking "What? What did you say?" Finally, she looked at me and with a tinge of agitation in her voice, she barked out, "Would you quit mumbling!"

I glanced her way giving her "the look," before proclaiming, "Would you be quiet, I'm trying to pray!" I know that I shouldn't have snapped at her, but trying to concentrate on two things at one time was especially difficult for me, especially when it was trying to drive in a blizzard and pray at the same time.

Not more than a few seconds after my little outburst, I saw something coming down the road in our direction. At first, it was just a dark, blurred silhouette. But, as it came closer, I could see it was a snowplow. When he saw us, he quickly pulled over to see if he could help. I jumped out of the car, running through the deepening snow as fast as I could.

Rolling down his window, he leaned out to ask, "Where you headed?"

"We're trying to get down Peoria to 113th Avenue," I yelled out in an effort to be heard above the noise of his diesel engine and the blowing snow.

He paused for a second then responded, "We're supposed to be keeping 120th open and we're having a hard time doing that. As soon as we plow it, the wind blows the snow back over it again, making it nearly impassable!" There was a trace of despair in his voice, and I could feel that he was as overwhelmed by the intensity of the storm as I was. After thinking about it for a minute he shouted out his window, "Get in your car and follow us. We'll plow down to 113th for ya!" I ran back to the car and hopped in. "Buckle up, he's going to plow down Peoria for us!" I shouted out with exuberance as I wiped the melting snow off my frosty face.

We started following the plow, and when we got to the point where we had to turn back before, the winds picked up with a vengeance, creating another complete whiteout. I slammed on the brakes, coming to a quick stop, since I couldn't see anything, including the snowplow. After a few minutes the snow let up just enough to see that the snowplow was leaning at a pretty steep angle. The whiteout had caused him to slide off the road into the ditch. As he tried to work the truck, rocking back and forth from reverse to first gear, it was obvious that he was burying the truck deeper and deeper into the soft mud. When he finally gave up, the wheels were buried past the hubs, and he wasn't going anywhere.

I mustered up the energy to get out of the car one more time, to battle my way through the raging storm up to the truck. I stepped up onto the running board as the driver rolled down his window. "I'm sorry kid, but there's no way we're getting out of here!"

"What are you going to do?" I asked with a tinge of guilt in my voice.

"We'll just radio in for someone to come get us, and in the meantime, we'll just wait out the storm. There aren't any other trucks in the area to help us, so we'll just wait. The only other truck is trying to keep 132nd open and they were having as much trouble keeping up with things as we were. So, we're all just going to hunker down and hope that the storm lets up pretty soon!" he stated as a matter of fact, like this was just a routine part of his job!

My heart sank in total despair as I headed back to the car. "They're not going anywhere!" I quipped, as I got in the car looking back at the kids. "I guess the only thing left to do is see if we can make it up to Flo and Ron's house!" I muttered as I turned the car around one more time to head back in the same direction we had just came from. "Lord help us," I prayed as I pulled up to the barely visible stop sign on 120th Avenue. The storm had let up, allowing the visibility to increase just a little bit. Straining to see out the windshield, I thought I saw another silhouette of something coming closer toward us. "What's that?" I questioned with an intense curiosity.

"It looks like a snowplow!" Kristi cried out with excitement.

We couldn't believe our eyes as another snowplow was fast approaching. I had no idea where it had come from since the other driver told me that there were no other plows available to come help us out. It wasn't supposed to be there, but then again, I didn't care! When it pulled up beside us, I quickly jumped out of the car into knee-deep snow and ran up to the driver's side of the plow as the man inside rolled down the window. I stepped up on the running boards as the driver leaned out the window to yell out, "Where you headed?"

"We're trying to get down Peoria to 113th," I eagerly replied as the windblown snow continued to fall sideways.

"Well, get in your car and follow us!" He replied with a reassuring smile.

I ran back to the car and jumped in, as Kristi anxiously asked, "What did he say?"

"He said to follow him!" I responded with a hopeful voice.

I knew we were going to finally make it there this time, I really did. I just knew it! God doesn't send help your way that many times without making sure you get where you're going. We followed the plow down Peoria until we reached 113th Avenue where the folks lived. The plow continued down Peoria as I gunned the engine on our little Toyota Corolla in an effort to blast through the drifted snow as far as we could before getting stuck. We ended up about twenty feet from the back fence of my parents' two-acre lot. We grabbed the sleeping bags, stuffed the kids in them, and then proceeded to head out in the blizzard for the last four-hundred feet of our arctic expedition.

Mom and Dad had been watching from their sliding-glass door with frantic anticipation. When they first saw a blurred shape of two people walking toward their house in the blowing cold, they quickly came running out to greet us. We had just crossed the three-rail fence when they met us. Dad grabbed Dennis from Kristi as we trudged through the thigh-deep snow drifts heading back to the house. Once inside, Mom and Dad hugged us like they would never let go. I have never been so thankful to be home. The love, the security that had always been a stable part of my life, was magnified to the nth degree as we stood in the kitchen, reliving the past three-and-a-half-hour journey.

After waiting an hour for us to arrive that morning, the folks started to worry as the snow quickly piled up around the area. Dad decided to take his truck out to find us. Less than a half-a-mile from the house, he had gotten stuck and had to walk back home himself in the raging blizzard. While Dad was out looking for us, Mom had started calling all the relatives to start a prayer chain for our safe return, as well as, for my brother Danny who had to work that morning. His four-wheel-drive Bronco had slid off the road, getting stuck right outside of the city on his way back home. But fortunately, he was able to walk several miles to his girlfriend Pam's house. He had called several hours earlier to let the folks know that he was okay. So all their concern and focused prayer had turned to us. I'm sure it took all the collective prayer to accomplish the miracle we had just experienced. As we stood around in the kitchen, discussing the miraculous rescue, I glanced out the sliding-glass door, to watch the snowplow head the opposite direction down Peoria, returning to wherever it came from. Within minutes the storm became so intense that we could no longer see anything beyond the back deck of the house. It was a total whiteout as the blizzard's intensity continued to increase.

I was convinced that God intervened to save us from that deadly, winter storm. The second snowplow should never have been in the vicinity to come to our rescue and safely guide us home. In fact, Dad still swears that he never saw a snowplow going down Peoria that morning. The only thing he ever saw was our tiny little brown car as we turned on 113th Avenue. The next day when Dad walked back to get his snowbound truck to bring it back home, he noticed that Peoria had never been plowed at all. In fact, his truck was stuck right in the middle of the road and there was no snow plowed up on either side of his truck. The only snow that surrounded his truck were the three-foot drifts that had swirled around this vehicular snow fence.

The snow chains that I had put on our car before we left home that morning lasted our entire drive; that is until we had been delivered to the back door of the folks' house. Both of them broke just as we high-centered on the snow drift right by the acreage. Without chains that little car would have never made it even half-way to our destination. It was amazing that even Danny's four-wheel drive Bronco only made it a few miles out of the city, while our rear-wheel drive Toyota carried us all the way home. Danny's story too was a miracle in itself as he was able to safely walk to a safe shelter from the storm. If he had gone any further, he would have been caught out in a merciless blizzard without any gear to survive, or even to stay warm. God's guardian angels were working overtime that day in their efforts to keep us safe in the midst of this deadly torrent of nature.

What gifts did we receive on that Christmas Day? We were given the gift of life which came through a miraculous deliverance. Prayers had been answered. I experienced a once-in-a lifetime opportunity as we were delivered out of a life-threatening storm by an angel of God. I still like to think that the two individuals in that second snowplow were angels. I often tell people that I had the opportunity to meet my personal guardian angels, and they both wore plaid. Even though we weren't all home together with Mom and Dad on that Christmas Eve, it was one of the most blessed celebrations I've ever experienced. Danny made it home the next day, while Randy and his family made it down from Snyder the next weekend so that we could celebrate in the traditional way, with a family feast and a gift exchange. By far, it was a Christmas celebration that allowed us to be touched by the mighty hand of God.

After I had finished telling Tim this story, I looked over at him to say, "But the greatest gift I received on that particular Christmas Eve, is the assurance that things are never hopeless. No matter how bleak things appear, there is always hope! God is always there, watching over our daily affairs. He has given His angels charge over us! We are always in His care!" As Tim and I exchanged a thoughtful glance, I noticed his cancer-scarred face, but I could also see the hope in his eyes as he responded, "I know!"

It was on the way back to Don's house, on the same road that I had traveled through that blizzard, that our conversations finally turned back toward the future. We talked about the challenge of what was fast approaching, and the impact it would have on all the family. It was at that moment, Tim told me in no uncertain terms, "I am ready to die! I have accomplished everything in this life that I was supposed to do. I have made sure that Timmy and Sue have accepted Christ as their Savior. I'm sure that my sisters and family also know Him." He paused for a moment before continuing, "I'm confident that all the ones I love will meet me someday in heaven. There is nothing else left to do in this life! I'm ready to go home!"

There was a moment of silent reflection as I sat there contemplating what Tim had just shared, as well as, the confidence with which he said it. I wasn't sure how to respond, in fact, I can't remember any of the final conversation as we traveled back to Don's house. I do remember the afternoon sun shining bright into my vehicle as we headed west toward the town of Golden. I also remember dreading the end of this special day! I knew there would never be another one like it as long as I lived.

As we pulled up in front of Don's house, I knew that our day was quickly coming to an end. I took one last look at Tim before he got out to slowly make his way up to the house. I walked with him up to the porch, where Don greeted us with a hearty grin, inviting me to come on in to visit for a bit. We shared all the highlights of the day, reliving the moments with animated gestures and laughter.

We pulled out our picture from the old-time photo parlor, laughing and carrying on like a couple of giddy school boys. It was with great reluctance that I bid them all farewell that evening. Even though Tim was completely exhausted, he insisted on walking me back out to my SUV. He thanked me for coming to get him, and for the fun we had shared that day. As I shook his hand I could feel the tears welling up in my eyes. "I'll see ya later," I said as I crawled into the vehicle. I buckled myself in before shutting the door.

Tim leaned forward, putting his hand on the door at the base of the rolled-down window. "Drive careful!" he said as I started the engine, putting the car in gear to begin to drive away.

Looking back in the rear-view mirror, I could see Tim still standing there, a shadowy figure engulfed in the effervescent rays of the setting sun. It reminded me of the picture I had hanging in my living room. The Indian brave, slumped on the back of his horse, his spear dangling loose under his arm. The horse's reins dangled from the warrior's hands, allowing the horse to hang its head low toward the ground in total exhaustion. The sun's golden rays softly silhouetted this young battered warrior as it gently descended beyond the rolling foothills. The reality of the moment nearly overwhelmed me as I realized the sun was quickly setting on a very special life. "It is the 'End of the Trail,'" I thought to myself as the tears flowed freely down my cheeks.

The sun does rise, the sun does set, the moon shines bright at night;
God saw the "day" that He had made, and knew that it was right . . .
Memories days, nostalgic days, days when one must ponder,
Of times now past, days long gone, "What is this life?" we wonder . . .
Shocking days, Denial days, what fate life holds in store;
The heart cries out in agony, reaching deep within its core.
Days of anger, unbelief, grasping out at straws,
Seeking for the "answers," searching for the cause.
Days of hurt and stress-filled days, the soul sinks, oh, so low,
Reach out to touch the hand of Him, Who shares our every woe.
Days of turning all to Him, Who knows our every need;
He sees the future from the past, "The Shepherd," He will lead.
"Not my will, but Thine alone," This is the prayer we pray,
Grant us courage, strength and faith, to see us through the day.
Precious days, fragile days, Life is now—today,
Yesterday's gone, tomorrow not come, forever? A breath away.
Days of support, of reaching out, to draw all loved ones 'round,
To share the message of the "faith," Greater love cannot be found.
Days of living close to God, 'Mid miracles and dreams,
Affirming deep commitments, eternal peace it brings.
Final days together, in communion, rich and sweet;
Leaving footprints in the sand, 'Til once again we meet.
Days of watching the setting sun, as the tears are softly flowing,
The final moment when day is done? There is no way of knowing . . .

—Clarice D. Cook

CHAPTER 7

To Take the Wings of the Dawn

The summer had flown by quickly, and the locusts' songs reminded me of fall's impending arrival. Where had the summer gone? Between coaching little league baseball and taking summer classes at the college, it didn't feel like I had taken any time off from teaching. The nights were beginning to cool off, while the days were getting shorter as I embraced those last few moments that the Indian summer had to offer. The past year had flown by so fast it seemed like a complete blur, a distant dream. So many things had happened that at times it was hard to differentiate between my imagination and reality. Yet, reality was, once again, rearing its ugly head as I prepared to begin another school year. With summer days waning, I had to prepare myself mentally for another year of emotionally charged challenges that teaching high school students required.

Being a single dad and a professional required a major juggling act as soon as fall classes began. Dropping the kids off at the before-school program, making sure to have someone there to pick them up, or fly out of the high school to speed over to their school so that I was there to pick them up was a constant challenge. Since the kids lived with me most of the time, that was one responsibility that landed squarely on my shoulders. Throw in things like after-school meetings, preparing meals, doing laundry, going shopping, cleaning house, and all the other variables of living alone with two children, and it becomes apparent that one needs to be mentally and physically prepared every day. Each day was like a race. The starter gun went off with the alarm every morning at 5:30 a.m. and the final flag wasn't thrown at the finish line until around 10:30 p.m. after each marathon day. By the time Friday rolled around I was usually just about beat. Every other weekend when the kids would go over to their moms, or the one day a week when they would spend the night with her was always a welcome relief. During those times, I could either sit around the house to relax, or as was the case quite often, I could go out on a date with a lady friend.

There was a lot of excitement in the family that fall since Tim's niece, Kimmie Sue as we called her, was getting married. Kim was not only a real sweetheart, but she was a really cutie, too! There's a distinction between beauty and cute, at least in my estimation. Beauty is one of those traits that usually only goes down about three layers, "epidermally" speaking. Cute is something that goes clear down to the very depths of the heart. Now I'm not saying that Kim wasn't good looking. In fact, she is truly beautiful. But, her beauty didn't stop at the seventh layer of skin like so many women, hers went clear to the bone. She never felt like a second cousin to me, as I loved her like a sister, in the same way I always thought of her Aunt Billee. Kim was with us on almost all of those family outings and excursions that we took growing up. Since she was about ten years younger than us, we always looked after her as if she was that little sister none of us ever had. We always showered her with hugs and attention and in return, she blessed us with her sweet, bubbly disposition.

It was hard to believe that Kim was old enough to be getting married, even though she had actually waited a few years longer than most blushing brides. From the time her announcement arrived, I could hear my Grandma William's voice declaring, "Where has the time gone?" I don't think that anyone grasps the real context of time until you become a parent, watching your children's lives become a perpetual hourglass indicating the passing of time, which of course, provides a profound sense of your own mortality. Watching all of my kids' shenanigans and various activities while they were growing up caused me to reflect on my own childhood since I did many of the same things. But then, when the grandkids come along, it seems like the sands of the hourglass trickle down at an exponential rate.

Memories, however, provide a different perspective to life in relation to time. As they are stored within our minds, those memories, in a way, provide a sense of agelessness. It's almost a glimpse of eternity as I think back to many of the memories of my childhood. The most significant ones all feel like they just happened yesterday. While the world around us is constantly changing or moving forward, memories defy the confines of time and space. Maybe this phenomenon is attributable to the possibility that memories of special moments are locked away in timeless images of eternal youthfulness deep within our souls. The human body, as well as the mind, has a tendency to slow down as age takes its toll, while the human soul never seems to show signs of aging. The very part of us who makes us who we are—the essence of our inner being—the reflection of "self" remains constant through life, never growing old. It makes me wonder if this part of us is the trait that goes with us into eternity.

Kim was marrying a young man named Scott, whom I always referred to as the "Music Man." He was quite the harmonica player, but he made a living running his own recording studio, and he was the master of the electronic recording world. He was a true artisan of the ever-changing technology of the recording industry. The few times I had been at his studio, recording some music for our church, I was amazed at what he was able to do within the intricacies of his recording technology. The control center where he would blend, mix, and fine tune the recordings looked like it belonged at the Kennedy Space Center. Scott is an impressive man, with a burly build, who proudly wore a neatly trimmed beard that made him look like a Victorian dignitary. Scott is one of the nicest, caring individuals I've ever met. Even though he reminds me of a gentle giant who wouldn't harm a fly, I always thought it would scare me to death to run into him in a dark alley. Kim and Scott had asked Danny and I to serve as ushers at their wedding, which was a thrill for both of us. I don't know anybody who would have ever been able to say no to Kim. But regardless, we were both anxiously waiting for that September day to roll around for our sweet Kimmie Sue to begin her life with a fine man named Scott.

Once again, it was like our prayers had been answered as this special day rolled around, because Tim was still with us. It meant the world to him to see Kim get married. Over the past year, Tim and I often reminisced over the times we watched over Kim, whether it was on one of our outdoor adventures at the lake, or even just in the daily routine of life. When she was a baby, Billee, Tim and I would take turns feeding her, changing diapers, or chasing after her when she began to crawl and get around. I still remember the very first time I got to hold her. It was quite the honor for me as I stared into her baby blue eyes, while rubbing the back of my finger softly across her rosy, red cheeks. She was the perfect baby, almost like a little china-doll. Whenever we would all go somewhere together, we would take turns carrying her around. There were many times when she would fall fast asleep in my arms as we would sit in the back seat of the car to head for home. Of course, this was long before laws were passed requiring babies and children to ride in car seats. In fact, car seats hadn't even been invented yet, but then again, neither had padded dash boards, seat belts with shoulder straps, or collapsible steering columns.

Tim always referred to me as Uncle Lanny, even though I was only a cousin to Kim. I never gave it much thought one way or another though. I enjoyed being a close cousin to Kim. Tim really was her uncle, and he had a special relationship with Kim. Although, with his easy-going personality, Tim had a special relationship with everybody. He was always more concerned about others than he was about himself, and it was blatantly obvious. He was always willing to lend a helping hand or give what he could if someone was in need. That was just one of his many traits that made him special to so many people.

The day of the wedding rehearsal was hot and unbearable as the afternoon sun was beating down on everyone who stood outside the church waiting for the rehearsal to begin. Danny and I meandered into the church, standing in the back just behind the last pew as we carried on a conversation with Aunt Dorothy and Billee. In the midst of our conversation, I caught a glimpse of Tim and Sue walking in one of the side doors near the front of the church. Billee had noticed them at the same time, and the horror on her face became a reflection of my own, as none of us could believe our eyes. Tim had deteriorated quickly over the few weeks since I had seen him last. It was obvious that the angel of death was drawing near to my beloved friend. He looked like an eighty-year-old man. His clothes were hanging loose off his emaciated frame. This once virile, young man shuffled along trying to maintain his balance by holding on to the front pew with a shaky, unsteady hand.

It had only been a few short weeks since we had shared that day in the mountains. But now, his complexion was extremely dark, almost a grayish black, while the moles on his neck and face had grown larger, protruding even farther out making them more pronounced and noticeable. In fact, dozens of moles were literally scattered across the exposed skin of his head and neck. Billee and I both had to turn away for a minute to gain our composure before we could go up to greet him in a way that wouldn't let on to our growing grief. Both of us had to take a moment to clear tears from our eyes and take a deep, calming breath. I wiped all indications of the salty stream of anguish from my cheeks as I continued to calm myself. It took several minutes to squelch the torment that ached within the depths of my innermost being as I prepared to walk toward the front of the church to greet Tim. Of course, he was tickled to see us, greeting us with his usual upbeat demeanor despite the obvious progression of his illness and the difficulty with which he walked into the sanctuary. With his typical humor, he made a few wisecracks that cut the tension in the air, which made us relax a bit. For the first time since this ordeal began, I was having trouble finding something to say. My own inhibitions were haunting me. My ability to carry on a conversation had completely vanished. When the minister made his way up to the front to begin the rehearsal, it provided a welcome distraction from the reality of Tim's condition.

After the rehearsal, the wedding party made their way to a posh hotel for the traditional dinner. I had never been a part of a wedding party where such a fine rehearsal dinner was provided. Brian and Dennis were with Danny and myself as we ended up sitting at the same table with Tim, Sue and Timmy. All of us that night knew that there was an unwanted guest joining us, as the face of death had permeated Tim's physical appearance. However, it didn't hamper his attitude, or his sense of humor. I was reminded of a verse in the 23rd Psalm contained in the Old Testament, written thousands of years earlier, "You prepare a table before me, in the presence of my enemies . . . " Everyone knew that night that Tim was facing the greatest of all human enemies—death. He was there in our midst, but even so we still had hope. Through our relationship with Jesus, we would be able to face this final enemy with confidence.

As we shared the meal that evening, stuffing ourselves with the delectable food prepared specifically for that wondrous occasion, I was reminded of a promise that God has made to everyone who knows Him. A great wedding supper will be prepared for everyone who calls upon the name of Jesus and allows Him to enter their lives to dine with Him. Revelation 19:9 NASB says this, "Blessed are those who are invited to the marriage feast of the Lamb!" I truly believe that promise! I believe there will come a time after each believer in Christ has "taken the wings of the dawn," when we will gather together for the greatest of marriage feasts. What an amazing occasion that will be, but it will never happen until we leave this Earth and stand in our Creator's presence. Until that time arrives, each of us must face the harsh realities of this life. As we enjoyed the excellent food that evening, the moment's reality tainted its pleasure, constantly reminding me that the things of this world will never compare to the things God has in store for us when He calls us home.

What became obvious during the night was that Tim was quickly deteriorating both physically and mentally. The prescribed morphine was causing him to have mild hallucinations. In a disturbing way, it was pretty funny, causing Tim to laugh at himself quite a bit when he would realize he had just made some off the wall comment. During part of the conversation, Tim abruptly changed the subject to ask me if I'd seen his new car. I looked at Sue with a bit of surprise, before asking, "Oh, you bought a new car?" Sue rolled her eyes, then shrugged her shoulders in a silent response. "So, where is it?" I asked Tim. "In the living room!" He replied with total seriousness.

Everyone broke out in laughter, including Tim, as he provided a disclaimer, "Sometimes I say things that don't make much sense. It's the morphine, so just ignore me if I don't make sense!"

Sue then shared some of the things Tim had been seeing or hearing. Things like monkeys in the living room and Tim answering the phone when it hadn't rung. Tim just chuckled as Sue shared some of his drug-induced shenanigans. Tim laughed again as he added to the conversation, "The living room was just covered with those little monkeys!" We all giggled a bit, but down deep I couldn't believe the hurt I felt in my heart. It was one of the most heart-wrenching nights of my life.

Tim and Sue didn't stay at the table too long after we were done eating. It was obvious that Tim was totally exhausted, so they decided to head up to their room at the hotel. Before they left the table, Tim invited us to come up before we headed home. We watched as Sue held onto his arm to lead him out of the dining room with Timmy trailing not too far behind. I looked over at Uncle Don as his eyes followed them out of the room. I could see the anguish and the helpless despair of a man who was losing his only son. The sparkle was gone out of his eyes, replaced by utter hopelessness. I thought about how God must have felt when His only Son was crucified on Calvary's cross. For in Jesus' final moments, He cried out in anguish and despair, "My God, My God, why have You forsaken Me?" (Matthew 27:46).

The feelings that permeated God's very being as He watched His Son suffer and die, must have been similar to the same feelings Don experienced watching Tim suffer and die. But we are given hope because of Jesus' sacrifice on that cross. He rose from the grave, conquering sin and death. Death is not the final factor in life. Death does not have the victory! Even still, watching your child battle for life is the ultimate heartbreak for any parent.

How much it must hurt to see your child losing such a battle. It goes against the very nature of life itself. Children should be the ones to walk their parents to the grave, not the other way around. It can be so difficult to let go of the most important things in your life. To trust in a God who we can't see with our eyes, but see only through our faith. Only through faith can we let go of a situation because we realize that we have no control. After you've done everything possible to make things right, the only other option available is to let it go to the Lord. I can't imagine how difficult it is for a parent to lose a child; I'm sure there is nothing in this life to compare it to. Watching someone in the prime of their life come up on the losing end of a battle with cancer or any illness makes a parent feel totally helpless. I could see it in Don's eyes. I could see it in Dorothy's face. Every expression, every look, every movement conveyed hopeless anguish, and conveyed the dread of their imminent loss.

Danny, the kids, and I went up to Tim and Sue's room for a few minutes after we finished dessert. We talked about lots of superficial things, our recent trip to Heritage Square, the weather, the wedding rehearsal, things that required no emotional response. The trivial rhetoric bounced around the room as we cautiously avoided subjects that would bring us back to the reality of the moment. In many ways, we didn't talk about anything at all that night since we were all somewhere else far from that place, in another time, in a happier locale. Maybe in some ways we were all suffering from the side effect of a natural morphine which numbed the reality of the situation. Whether we wanted to admit it or not, all of us were in a bit of denial that destiny was fast approaching on the not-so-distant horizon.

The wedding wasn't the typical matrimonial affair, at least not any that I had ever attended. Only in my beloved Aunt Dorothy's family could the bride be late to her own wedding, and I'm not just talking about being fashionably late. As ushers, Danny and I were responsible for seating the multitude of guests according to their designated relational ties, sort of the original version of "his and hers," or maybe "the Hatfields and McCoys." I'm not sure. In this case however it was more of a game of hurry up, find a seat, then wait! And wait! And wait! It appeared like the wedding party should start providing some type of pre-game entertainment. Maybe lead a sing-along, or do a soft-shoe rendition of "*Dancing in the Rain.*" Maybe we could have a talent show, or a game show, like *Family Feud.* Since we were in a church, maybe we could start up a game of "Wedding Bingo," or a little Karaoke. But after sitting there waiting for what seemed like an eternity, I was leaning toward putting together a friendly little pool for people to pick the exact time that the bride might show up. The winner could take half the pot, and the wedding party (in waiting) could divvy up the other half. But, our better judgment prevailed and our good senses kicked in as we just stood in the back of the church, pacing like expectant fathers, to wait in an uncharacteristic dignified manner.

It seems that Dorothy had taken Kim to have her hair done in Boulder, a college town not too far from Denver. Well, not too far on any normal day. The thirty-six-mile trip was exacerbated by the fact it was Saturday afternoon, and Colorado University would play a football game against its rival, the Nebraska Cornhuskers. The game at Folsom Stadium in Boulder was scheduled to start at the same time as the wedding, which of course caused a traffic jam of epic proportions leading both in and out of the quaint college town. It amazed everyone that Kim would go to Boulder on that particular day, but then again, since nobody in the wedding party was a collegiate fan, the thought probably never entered anyone's mind to take that game and its locale into consideration. Dad had always joked around that Dorothy would be late to her own funeral, and so, apparently, the late gene had been carried on down into her grandchildren.

The strain of the situation was beginning to take its toll on Scott who was waiting in the wings, sweating like he was in a sauna, pacing like a caged lion. I'm sure he was beginning to wonder if he was going to be the jilted groom, left waiting at the altar. It's amazing how cruel guys can be who are all dressed up in their best tuxedo with no place to go and nothing to do. So, for a bit, teasing and left-at-the-altar jokes went flying, that is until we could see that they were about to take their toll on poor Scott. Then we enlightened him that being tardy to an event was a long-practiced family trait, at least, as far as Dorothy was concerned. It really was her *modus operandi*. Everyone knew that if you wanted Dorothy to be somewhere at 1:00 p.m., you told her to be there at 12:00 a.m. And then of course, she'd still be a few minutes late.

Kim was about thirty minutes late to her own wedding, and even though she wouldn't admit it, I still think maybe it was planned to make her entrance that much more dramatic and suspenseful. It was a beautiful wedding. Kim was an exquisite bride. Although Scott cleaned up pretty well himself, too. It was a day of great celebration as we shared the dream of a bright and loving future for a very special couple. Again, it was one of those times in life that cause a person to reflect on hopes, dreams and thoughts about the future. As the ceremony continued on, I looked over toward Tim as he sat in that wooden pew, hands folded in his lap in an almost prayerful meditation. I knew without a shadow of a doubt, after the many intimate conversations between us, that he was ready to meet his Maker. As I sat there in the peace of the moment, I was sure that he was lifting his eyes toward the heavens in anticipation of his homecoming.

Tim had prepared his life for this point in time, when he knew that he would soon be standing before the Creator of Life. As the Apostle Paul wrote, "Be sober in all things, endure hardship, do the work of an evangelist, fulfill your ministry. For I am already being poured out as a drink offering, and the time of my departure has come. I have fought the good fight, I have finished the course, I have kept the faith" (2 Timothy 4:5-8).

Tim had kept the faith. Oh, how he had kept the faith. In fact, I had never seen it waiver since the moment this ordeal began. Was it irony or God's infinite wisdom that those verses popped into my head that day, especially since they came from the book of Second Timothy?

Over the past year so much had happened. Much of which could be considered coincidence, but personally, I know it was a personal touch from our Master's hand, within the design of His divine plan. Is it a coincidence when something happens at just the right moment in the unending expanse of time? Or, is it God working in our lives? Personally, I'm sure these divine "coincidences" are proof that God is intimately involved in our lives. To me, they serve as a message to make note of, since they show He is in control of life, even though at times it seems to spin completely out-of-control. Through everything that we had experienced up to that point in time, God was there for each of us. The message He wants us to hear as He shows up to meet us in our hour of need, doesn't become evident through a booming, thunderous voice, rolling through the heavens. But, instead, we hear God's voice, and feel His presence, when we silence our hearts to listen. Then, like the wind whispering through the leaves of a tree, we can hear Him. There was an inscription in the church that Tim and I attended as teenagers which provided a light that guided us through all of the challenges of life. It was from the book of Psalms and it read, "Be still and know that I am God!" As I stood silently as a witness to this sacred ceremony of holy matrimony; a ceremony that symbolized God's unconditional love, I stilled my heart, and cleared my mind as I embraced the very presence of God Himself.

The reception was held at the Heatheridge Country Club, a rather ritzy place to which I wasn't accustomed. But there was food, drink, dancing, and as the saying goes, "plenty of merriment." Tim was surrounded by old friends, standing around sharing stories of times nearly forgotten. People came whom we hadn't seen in years, for instance, friends of the family that we used to go skiing with, as well as distant relatives like the kind you only see at a wedding or a funeral. The place was abuzz with the chattering of long-lost acquaintances who had once been a part of our younger years and who were catching up on the times that had passed.

After awhile Tim made his way over to my table, pulling out a chair to sit down next to me. "How's it going?" I inquired.

"Alright, I guess," he replied with a slight hesitation.

"It looks like you're about worn out," I said in an effort to talk over the noise of the crowd and the blast of the music.

"I'm getting pretty tired," Tim confided.

We continued our conversation for some time, just chatting about the day's activities, along with how nice the wedding had been. Not too long into the conversation though, Tim leaned in close. While still looking me directly in the eyes, he confided that it bothered him how people were saying goodbye to him. They were saying it like they would never see him again, ever! It bothered him deeply that they couldn't see past the immediate future. He leaned in even closer as he said, "You know that we will see each other again. You know that, don't you?"

I stared deep into his nearly lifeless, brown eyes, and then replied, "Of course, I know that. I know that we will!"

When it was time to go, Tim got up to walk me out to my truck. "Where do you think you're going?" Sue called out with obvious concern for Tim.

"I'm going to walk Lanny to his truck!" he shouted back.

Sue wasn't going to allow Tim to go outside by himself in his morphine-induced state. "Timmy, go with your dad and keep an eye on him!" she whispered into Timmy's ear. It was obvious that she was concerned he would become disoriented, not able to remember where he was and not be able to find his way back into the reception. As we walked out toward the parking lot, I looked at Tim in an effort to remember as much about him as I could. I wanted to put to memory every last bit of this moment that was before me.

It was clear, I knew that it was almost over. I was sure that this would be our last walk together on the fertile soil of this Earth. I could understand why everyone was telling Tim goodbye with such finality. Yet, I was confident that this wouldn't be the end of his walk. I knew; I was confident that he would just step through another door, into a world filled with the wonders of God's promise as he followed the light of Jesus that will lead all of us into eternity. Stepping outside of the doors of that country club was one of the most difficult things I have ever done. I knew that this trail had ended. I looked into Tim's cancer-scarred face, deep into his nearly lifeless eyes, and I said, "I'll be seeing you, Tim!"

We started out giving each other a handshake, but it quickly turned into a long embrace with our arms tightly secured around each other. I realized that this was the first time in our lives that we had ever given each other a hug. "I'll see ya!" Tim said before adding, "You take care of yourself!" With that lasting embrace behind us, I reluctantly got into my truck and rolled down the window. "Drive safe!" Tim added as I started to drive away, waving good-bye!

As I drove out of the parking lot, I remembered the words of a dear friend, "Let go and let God!" At that instant, I realized that Tim had conquered the greatest sin of all. The only one of the Deadly Sins that has eternal consequences. Deadly Sin Number Seven, not only of childhood, but for all ages, "Living a life in denial of God" and His love for us. It was obvious, that the greatest sin anyone could ever commit, was living a life without faith in Jesus. The only unforgivable sin is to deny until death that Jesus died on the cross, rose from the grave, ascended into heaven, and sits at the right hand of God. To not accept God's gift of love through Jesus is to condemn our souls to eternal damnation. No matter how bleak things appear in this world, there is always hope when we turn our lives over to the loving care of Jesus.

It wasn't too long after the wedding when Mom called one afternoon to let me know that Tim had taken a turn for the worse. She said that Dorothy had gone down to Fort Morgan to see him and he was barely able to stay awake. Between the disease and the higher doses of pain medication, he was having a difficult time knowing what was going on. He was extremely weak and he was deteriorating rapidly. She continued to share what Tim had said to Dorothy as she was talking to him in his exhausted state. As Dorothy stood by his bedside, he lifted his eyes and quietly whispered, "Mom, I need to go to sleep now. I'm so tired from working all day!"

Dorothy laughed because she knew he had been sleeping all day. She leaned in close to him and asked, "What have you been working on?"

Tim opened his eyes, to reply, "I've been painting butterflies for you."

I'm sure that his words brought immediate tears to his loving mother's eyes. Dorothy had always loved butterflies. From the earliest time I could remember, she was fascinated by these most delicate of God's creatures. She always displayed various butterfly decorations throughout her house. Golden butterflies were on her walls, and real butterfly wings were in her coasters. Butterflies, most of which were arrangements that she had created or even painted herself, adorned nearly every flower arrangement and piece of art inside her home.

Was Tim dreaming about painting butterflies, or was he bringing back a message of hope from somewhere between this life and the next? I think that he was beginning to see past the curtain that veils this life from the hereafter. It seemed that he was beginning to hover in the expanse that leads to eternity. It's possible that his soul was beginning to float back and forth between the heavenly gates of paradise and this world, like a butterfly emerging from its cocoon. I could never say for sure, but no matter what anybody thought, it was clear that Tim was about to step into the promise of God's eternal paradise.

It was only a few days later when Tim was placed in a hospice in Fort Morgan, because Sue could no longer provide for his medical needs. I waffled back and forth with a desire to go down to visit him. A part of me longed to see him, but another part wanted to remember him the way I had seen him over the last few months. I wanted an unblemished memory instead of an image of cancerous growths that had completely taken over his body. A growth on his neck had developed so quickly and grown so large that it was difficult for him to breathe, and impossible for him to speak. I knew we were both aware that we had seen each other for the last time in this life. I drew comfort from our final meeting at Kim's wedding.

I was standing in the office at school when Randy walked into the room and motioned me to follow him into the back room. It was during the five-minute passing period between classes, and I knew by his expression what the news would be. I realized that Tim's battle was over and that he had crossed into glory. I don't remember any of that conversation, but it didn't matter, I knew Tim had gone home. It was October 3, 1989—he was thirty-two-years old. I couldn't cry, although my heart was breaking. I just couldn't let the tears flow at that moment since I had to finish teaching classes for the day.

That night, I went over to Dorothy's to spend time with many of the people that Tim loved. Billee and I stood in the kitchen with our arms tightly secured around each other while the tears flowed gently down our cheeks. Softly, she whispered the story of his last few hours. Surrounded by his immediate family, they sang one of his favorite hymns, "The Old Rugged Cross," and then one of his favorite children's worship songs, "This Little Light of Mine." The family took turns holding his hand and Billee described how a tear rolled down his cheek when Sue held baby Chad next to him to give him a kiss. Tim kept lifting his hand up toward the ceiling, which upset Don as he kept instructing the family to put his hand down so that he could save his energy. Don was having a terrible time accepting the loss of his son. Through it all, Tim continued to stretch his arm out toward the ceiling. Finally, Billee realized what he was doing. "Do you see Jesus?" She asked. Tim replied with a nod.

Jesus was there, waiting on the other side of the veil that we're not allowed to see beyond. His arm went limp, and as his final breath expended from his lungs, the part of his being that made him Tim, left his shell of a body as he reached up to grasp the hand of Jesus. Tim was gone. He stepped through the gates that separate this life from eternity as he took the "wings of the dawn." Tim had left us with our tears. He had left us with our memories. Tim had left us with the hope of meeting him on that distant shore that lies beyond our human comprehension. We would all meet again someday when the trumpet sounds and Jesus calls the rest of us home. God was gracious. When the doctors said he only had a few months to live, he was given a year. We were allowed the opportunity to prepare ourselves for life without this very special man.

The day of Tim's funeral I drove down to Fort Morgan by myself. I needed to be alone with my thoughts as I needed time to remember and to reflect on life. I listened to the song "I'd Rather Have Jesus," then I'd rewind the tape to listen to it again. The entire trip to Morgan, I listened to that one song. While I felt remorse, engulfed by the ache of loss which radiated from my innermost being, I recalled the words of the Apostle Paul contained in the book of First Corinthians 15:55 NASB, "O, grave, where is your victory, O death where is your sting?" I still had a hope. I still knew that there would be a tomorrow for all of us who call on the name of Jesus, and who follow His path.

I was honored to serve as a pallbearer for Tim's casket, along with my brothers Randy and Danny, my cousin Rick and Tim's two brothers-in-law. I thought it was appropriate that those of us who shared so much with Tim in this life, be allowed to take his remains to their final resting place. Tim and I literally carried each other through this life. It meant so much to be able to carry him one last time. I had a sense that somehow Tim was still with me. The essence of his life would be with me until my dying day. He had touched my life in so many ways; we played together, we fought at times, and we even enjoyed some pretty intense rivalries. But, we were always there for each other, even during those times when it was just in spirit. We had touched each other's very souls and we would always be a part of each other. We were destined to be "Buddies forever!"

I don't remember much about Tim's service. They sang two of his favorite songs, "The Old Rugged Cross," and "Just a Closer Walk with Thee." They read one of his favorite poems, "Footprints." During the message, I only remember thinking back to the good times, pondering the circumstances that brought us to this point. At the time, my mind was swirling so fast I thought I would pass out. I had to sit back to take several deep breaths so I wouldn't hyperventilate. Even though I knew Tim was now taking his place in God's heavenly kingdom, my heart ached for the passing of my closest, earthly friend.

Mom had written a poem about Tim in the few days preceding his service, after Dorothy had told her about Tim's butterflies. Mom has an amazing talent that few people possess. She can put into melodic rhymes the thoughts within her heart. The writings that she creates provide reflective thoughts of comfort and peace during times of despair that really seem like they come directly from the heart of God. Mom read her poem during the service and of course, there wasn't a dry eye in the place. I was amazed that she had the strength and the courage to be able to share those highly personal, poetic reflections during Tim's service.

Mom has always been an amazing role-model of her faith. If she hadn't been able to lean on Jesus during the reading of that poem, I know she could have never finished sharing it. Her writings have always been a reflection of God's love and His devotion to us. The poem she shared that day mirrored the love of Jesus that was manifested within the DNA of our family. I'd like to share just an excerpt from it.

"I'm Painting Butterflies for You!"

I'm painting butterflies for you,
    In orange and yellow, green and blue,
One for each before I go—
    To let you know I love you so,
Watch them flutter, watch them fly . . .
    Hurry now before I die.
Here's one for Sue, My darling wife,
    She brought sweet joy into my life.
She added laughter, days of fun,
    And bore my children, one by one;
She shared my burdens, eased my fears,
    And oft-time wiped away my tears;
We took our marriage vows to heart,
    Our promise stood 'till death do part;
It's finished now—this pretty one,
    Watch it fly up toward the sun . . .
Catch the rainbo's shimmering hue,
    Fly on my pretty; Sweet, sweet Sue.
Brush strokes with love—two lively ones,
    One for each of my two sons;
See them frolic, see them play,
    Having fun all through the day;
Little Tim named after me,
    A rambunctious burst of energy,
I've had the chance to nurture, feed,
    To guide his steps from infancy's seed,
I've shared his life 'till the day comes
    When I must leave my precious sons,

Not by choice, but by God's plan . . .
    There is no better way for man;
But ere I go I ask of you,
    If there is just one thing you'll do;
Tell my youngest, Baby Chad,
    All about his loving Dad . . .
When life is o'er and I am gone,
    Through my two sons, my seed lives on;
Fly on you playful butterflies
    Into life's future, sun-filled skies.
I'm painting this one, Mom for you . . .
    Only a perfect one will do;
See the Colors? Watch them shine—
    A radiant, darting valentine
Fluttering 'round all through my life,
    Thru joys or tears, peace or strife,
Never asking anything in return . . .
    A priceless crown, Dear Mom, you'll earn;
Henceforth, you see a butterfly,
    Just think it too, was once as I
Emerging from its warm cocoon,
    Like a baby from his mother's womb,
To live, to love, and then to die,
    Soaring toward heaven—it's not goodbye,
It's simply migration, for awhile . . .
    Now dry your tears, put on a smile,
I'm going to heaven, I've work to do,
    Painting more butterflies, Mom, for you!
I'm painting this one, huge and bold,
    If you look at it closely you'll see wings of gold,
Each color filled stroke makes me quite glad,
    I'm happy I'm painting this one for Dad,
'Twas Dad always making something for me,
    Mending repairing, building swings in a tree,
Fixin' flat tires, carving out toys,
    Dads have a special way with their boys;
By building and molding, new things begin,
    Following Dad's footsteps turn boys into men;
Look! Here's three I've finished in a row,
    Faces shining—a radiant glow,

Shadowed 'midst the colors bright,
    A glorious, wondrous, graceful sight.
Reminding me of days of yore,
    When we were the "Trusty Kids'" of four,
Spending our childhood days in glee,
    Not always in perfect harmony,
But love was the center of our lives,
    Through love even "Little Brother" survives;
To help build memories dear to your heart;
    Cherish them now when we must part;
"Let my light shine," keep singing along,
    Hum for me now my favorite song,
Then Cheri, and Laurie and Billee Dea,
    I'll greet you in heaven—"Just wait and see!"
Cousins by nature, by choice became friends,
    Buddies forever—not just when life ends.
We grew up together, drew close to each other,
    Three sisters by birth, I needed a brother!
We played and shared, we rivaled and vied,
    All through the years our friendship survived,
Childhood passed quickly-the years simply flew-
    Now Lanny my buddy, I paint one for you,
The blues of the heavens I'll paint on its wings,
    The freedom of eagles its rhapsody sings,
Reach for your life goals—spread your wings wide,
    Soar as an eagle in freedom and pride;
Conquer the world, make dreams come true,
    Remember my buddy I'm countin' on you.
I've big ones and small ones, yellow, white—
    Orange, red and blue, what a beautiful sight!
Now I'm so tired and I really must go,
    Just keep in mind I love you so,
"How," you ask, "do you know I do?"
    'Cause I painted butterflies just for you!
Okay, butterflies be on your way,
    Hasten now—please don't delay,
Send out the message life imparts:
    Transcending love heals broken hearts,
Unites our souls eternally,
    Unbinds our spirits—sets us free,

To live unfettered—free from sin,
In unity with God and men.
Now, ere you see a butterfly,
Catch it not—let it fly by
To dive and flutter, soaring high,
Upward, upward toward the sky,
Watch on until it's gone from sight,
Flying swiftly toward the light,
Catch the ethereal, airy hue . . .
I dip my wings—farewell to you.
Think oft of me, remember too,
I'm painting butterflies for you!

—Clarice D. Cook

The autumn sun seemed to bask us in its warmth as we carried his casket from the hearse to his grave. There was an amazing peace and tranquility out there on the edge of the prairie as the only sounds I remember hearing were those of the birds, singing their cheerful songs. "His eye is on the sparrow, and I know He watches me." The words from a song we used to sing as teenagers at church echoed through my mind. Standing there at the moment, it seemed like the world was standing still, pausing to reflect on a life lived to its fullest. Maybe the world didn't pause, but those of us who saw Tim to his final resting place took the time to pause—to reflect. I thought about one of the things Dorothy had shared, the evening after Tim had died. "His complexion was black when he came into this world, and it was black when he left it." It seemed like the cycle had made full circle. Tim was born in Fort Morgan and was rushed to Denver in an effort to save his fragile life. He returned to Fort Morgan as an adult, to live his life, making a home for himself and his family. He was sent back to Denver in an effort to save his life one more time. He returned home to Morgan, one last time, to die, and to be laid to rest. Irony? Maybe. But through it all, I see the touch of our loving Master's hand.

As they lowered his casket into the grave, I remembered a life that was just like mine. A life that had hopes and dreams, a life that was integrally connected to mine. I remembered a life that made a commitment to follow Jesus twenty years earlier on the side of a mountain in the Rockies. I finally saw the significance of that decision. I am so thankful for the people who made that camp possible. I am forever grateful that God gave us both an opportunity to know Him and that He reached out to share His love with us. There is a reassurance in knowing that God is always in control.

It hasn't been easy living life as a Christian. There were times when co-workers and even pseudo-friends ridiculed me for my convictions, especially working in the liberal public school system. In the liberal age that we live in, there are those who feel intimidated by the conservative views I hold because of my faith. But, Jesus never said that life would be easy. When He called us to "take up" our cross to follow Him, He knew that it wasn't an easy road to follow. In fact, He warned us that the world would be against us. The Apostle Paul gives us encouragement to the challenges that Christians face when he said, "If God is for us, who can be against us?" (Romans 8:31).

During this season of my life, the significance of living a life based on the foundation of Jesus' love and forgiveness was clearly evident. The seeds of faith that had been planted, watered and nurtured through the years had culminated on this sunny, autumn afternoon on the eastern plains.

As we reflected on Tim's life, one that was deeply rooted in the faith of Jesus, we were all reminded of the dreadful reality that life on Earth is finite, it will come to an end. Only through Jesus can hope shine through the devastation of grief and loss. This final trial in life that each of us will face someday, was the reason that Tim and I even considered the ultimate question about "What lies beyond this world?" The question that led to our spiritual awakening. At a little church camp in the mountains, twenty years earlier, we had made our reservations for the journey to heaven. We had looked into our futures at that Christian camp and wondered what our futures would hold. There among the tall, bristling pine trees, we contemplated the question of how we wanted to be remembered when we left this world. As the years flew by, it was one of the most important questions we would ever have to answer.

For Tim, his earthly future had come to a close, the culmination of those childhood years of growing and struggling in preparation for life had already paid off. In some ways, I was envious that Tim was leaving on an adventure without me. We had shared so many experiences together, and seen so many things that it didn't seem quite right that he was now sharing God's expanse of eternity firsthand, without me. He had stepped into eternity, yet it seemed that God still had plans for me in this world. I would have to carry on to experience different adventures without my lifelong friend by my side. But, just like the first time skiing, one of us would serve as an example in order to make the path a little smoother for the other.

I wondered what it was like, what Tim was seeing, what miraculous wonders he was now experiencing. However, I knew that someday, when the Lord was ready, I too would make that journey. To coin one of my favorite sayings, "When the Lord calls, there is no call waiting." I still had things to do in this world. Yet I also knew that I had to continue to prepare myself for that journey when it finally arrived, just as Tim had done. He was prepared to reach out to take the hand of Jesus as he entered into eternity. His life had prepared him for that moment, and in the process, his life had touched many lives in his final hours as he lived the faith that he held on to even unto death.

I will never forget the influence that Tim and I had on each other's lives. Every day that goes by, I remember some experience that we shared, some joke that we laughed at, and some prank that we pulled. Life in itself is an adventure. We were fortunate, we had Jesus guiding us through this adventure. He blessed us with many wonderful things, not only each other, but an amazing family. He gave us an unmerited gift, one we didn't deserve—one that there was no way we could earn. What we do with that gift after we receive it is nearly as important as the gift itself. What a waste to have this wonderful gift and not share it with our loved ones, or with those we encounter along life's way.

The sun does rise, the sun does set, the moon shines bright at night;
God saw the "day" that He had made, and knew that it was right . . .
Cloudy days, sunless days, Stroke softly as a feather,
The Creator masks the sting of death, thru times of stormy weather,
Days of sorrow, days of woe, Days so filled with grief,
Days that rip the heart apart, to test your faith's belief.
Healing days, peace-filled days, the heart with time does mend,
As Jesus takes away the hurt; He is our dearest friend.
Welcome days of the morning dawn, after the wings take flight;
Dipping, diving, soaring high, pursuing His radiant light.
Future days, heavenly days, Time will never sever,
The tie that binds not just for life . . . There buddies dwell forever.
Eternal days, glorious days, where "day" fades back to space;
There He will draw His children home, and greet them face to face.
To live with Him Forever, In that home beyond the skies,
Rich days of true contentment, in that land of paradise!

—Clarice D. Cook

CHAPTER 8

Life Continues On

It has been more than twenty-five years since I shared my last earthly encounter with Tim. Even still, there's seldom a day goes by that I don't think about my most special of friends. When my good friend Mary Arnold passed away, that experience renewed and energized a flood of memories that had been neatly packed away in my heart for years. However, some of those memories were ones I hadn't thought about for a long time. Not that they weren't sweet memories, it's just that so often the hectic pace of life requires our mind to file more distant memories into the archive. Only when something profound happens do these deeper memories resurface.

So much had happened over the past twenty-five years, truly life had moved on. Our kids had grown up, and most of them had gotten married. There are grandkids running all around much like we were more than fifty years ago. Both Dennis and Brian each have one son, although we also have four wonderful granddaughters evenly split between my two sons. The two grandsons are almost like a re-enactment of Tim and me as they have an amazing time tearing around making their own adventures whenever they have time together. Little Timmy is married with a family of his own and Baby Chad is no longer a baby, still living with his mother Sue. Sue however, never did remarry, but chose instead to focus on raising her two sons and working the small ranch that she bought not long after Tim passed away. As time has passed, all of the great-grandparents have gone home to be with the Lord, along with many of the relatives and friends who were a part of our skiing adventures.

I spent twenty-eight years working in the public school system, before retiring to pursue my second career as an associate pastor at my church. I remarried too, just a few days before I retired. I had spent nearly twenty years as a single father before taking the plunge to find marital bliss. All of our parents are still hanging in there, although it's difficult to see them arrive at the age that our grandparents were back in the day. I realized I was getting old when one day I woke up and the thought hit me that I was past the age that my parents were when I considered them to be in the prime of their life. What happened to the time? Where did it go? Finally, I understood my grandparent's perspective. In my memory, everything seems like it happened just yesterday, even though there's decades of memories locked away in my heart.

That last year of Tim's life had a significant impact on my own. Through that experience I realized that as a Christian, I just couldn't live life, I had to live life following Jesus. I have to admit, it's been an amazing journey, although I hope to continue on this sojourn for many more years before I hang up the old towel myself. During those years immediately following Tim's death, I started to actively pursue Jesus. I joined a church, got involved in the choir, became a part of the church leadership, started singing in a gospel group, and even had the opportunity to serve as a lay speaker within the little Methodist church that I faithfully attended with Brian and Dennis.

When God decided it was time for me to change directions, He orchestrated events that led me to a larger, non-denominational church where I became even more involved with serving in ministry. I started helping in the Single's Ministry, where I facilitated divorce care groups, and also taught single-parent classes. I started writing, had several books published, and then got involved with the church's drama ministry. There I started acting, then doing some writing, even helping direct a few skits and special drama productions. I joined the choir, and became part of the leadership team that planted a new church campus. Eventually, I was ordained as a pastor, and currently have the privilege of being an associate pastor in another church plant, overseeing various components of the ministry while helping others find a place to serve in the church. Now, I'm privileged to share the love of Christ with those in need, because part of my assignment requires me to do hospital and nursing home visits.

As I look back at the myriad experiences that I have encountered in this life, I'm amazed to see how every hurt, every bit of brokenness that I endured, God used to develop empathy for others as I became better equipped to provide encouragement to those encountering suffering and loss. After all, where else can you turn when you're flat on your back and the world seems to fall apart? The only place to turn is to the One who created you in the first place, the One who knit you together in your mother's womb! During the most trying times of your life, when circumstances seem unbearable, when you're too weak to carry on, those are the moments to lift your eyes toward the hills to see where our help comes from. When the seas are smooth and life is filled with blessings, we often turn away from Jesus' outstretched hands, ignoring His beckoning call. During those times we become too dependent upon our own strength, often boasting of our own ability to be self-sufficient and in control. But when the world comes crashing in, and when we lose total control of life, that is when we cry out for help from God above.

After serving in the capacity of an associate pastor, I had the opportunity to return to Camp Id-Ra-Ha-Je for a Family Camp. It had been more than forty years since I had visited the mountain retreat where my spiritual awakening commenced. We were only there for a couple of days, with about 100 adults and children in attendance. What an amazing experience it was to see both children and adults commit their lives to Christ. A dozen people accepted Jesus into their lives, then confirmed their choice to follow Jesus as they were baptized as an outward profession of their faith. The baptism took place in a makeshift baptismal, which was actually an animal water tank filled with fresh water. Somebody forgot to inquire about filling the tank with equal amounts of warm water mixed with cooler, mountain-spring run-off. Our campus pastor nearly turned blue from the chilled temperature of the water that day. Every person who emerged from that tank did so like they had just experienced a polar bear plunge. Later on, I teased the pastor that we shouldn't try to "freeze the sin out of our congregants." There had to be a better way. The next year, we made sure that part of the water came out of one of the camp's large hot water heaters, creating a much more comfortable experience.

Returning to the camp where my spiritual journey began was an experience that invigorated my faith. As I wandered through the camp, my memory was flooded with my time there with Tim. Much of the camp had barely changed, like the lodge where we spent our time, along with the cafeteria where I tried to force down that thick, sticky, raisin-filled oatmeal. The old fort was gone, but it was replaced with a new, amazing one with ten-foot walls, complete with watch towers and a rampart that overlooked the large wooden gate. This is where all the planned water fights now occur with water-balloons for the campers who spend a week at the camp. Apparently, the tradition that began with the first water fight at the camp when Tim and I were there created a long lasting, more-controlled tradition of liquid fun.

What I didn't realize at that time was that the camp had just begun operation only a few years before Tim and I attended that first summer. During my return visit as an adult, I discovered that the camp had a huge journal that contained the names of all the campers who had committed their lives to Jesus while at camp. They began keeping a record of those names a few years after Tim and I had attended. The first page recorded the year 1969, which was the inaugural year of the facility. Tim and I first attended the camp in 1971, so I was thrilled to add our names to the list for that year. Looking through the book brought tears to my eyes as I went through each year looking at the names of young people who were intimately impacted through the camp's activities and mission.

On the side of the hill, where we gathered around the bonfire to sing songs and listen to a message about Jesus, there still stood that wooden cross, made out of large pine logs. The actual place where my journey began was still there, exactly like I remembered it from forty years earlier. During my time at Family Camp, I was afforded an opportunity to once again reflect on my walk with Jesus. It was here that I'd committed my life to Him as a child, in that same spot, with the same stars glistening above in the night sky of the Rocky Mountains. My memory took me back in time to relive the moment—the smell of burning pine permeated the air, the crackling fire blazed with mesmerizing passion, causing me to stare into the brilliantly colored flames. The fire illuminated the large wooden cross, made out of giant pine logs. A glimmering, golden radiance amplified this symbolic monument of faith's significance. Embers and ash floated past silhouettes of moon-lit trees, disappearing in the vast, star-filled sky. What a blessing to revisit this place and reflect on that journey, begun as a teenager, from this pine-covered mountainside.

As I look back at my life from that vantage point, I couldn't help but be thankful that Jesus had found me on that mountainside decades earlier. I can't imagine what my life would have been without Him at the helm. There's a storm in every human heart that can only be calmed through a personal relationship with Jesus. My life has contained more storms than I care to remember, even several which could be considered the "perfect" storm. I would have never survived those storms if it hadn't have been for the relationship that I had developed with Jesus. There was the divorce, then the challenge of being a single parent until Brian and Dennis were adults, the death of Tim, the loss of grandparents and close friends, even the loss of my baby brother Gordon Lee; this life threw me a lot of curveballs. Without Jesus, I don't know if I would have been able to weather any of those storms, let alone all of them. I really have no idea how anyone can make it through this life without knowing Him.

Everybody trusts in something or someone for answers to the big issues. Throughout life we ponder questions such as "Why are we here?" "What is our purpose?" "What happens after we die?" "Is there life after death?" "Where will I spend eternity?" Humanity has an innate desire for eternal significance. We are created in the image of God and He placed that desire in each of us. It's like a compass that points us back to spiritual north, or back to God. "He has made everything beautiful in its time. He has also set eternity in the human heart; yet no one can fathom what God has done from beginning to end" (Ecclesiastes 3:11 NIV).

Throughout antiquity, from the moment humanity breathed in life-sustaining oxygen for the very first time, these questions have stirred within the hearts and minds of our ancestors. From the beginning of creation, man has pondered what lies beyond this life. The Egyptian and Roman cultures were preoccupied with life after death. The Egyptian pharaohs and the many Caesars of Rome proclaimed themselves to be gods while they were still alive. Caesar Augustus, who lived in the Roman Empire during Jesus' day, was a perfect example. Augustus used the Greek word "gospel" to describe his new world order. The empire declared him a god and established rites of worship proclaiming that his reign would last forever. There are religions today that believe in all kinds of roads that lead to their version of heaven. Some of these religions proclaim that certain members can become a god of their own little planet somewhere in a galaxy far-away while laying claim to a multitude of virgins who are guaranteed to make their planetary reign one of intimate pleasure and personal contentment.

Nearly all religions try to provide the answers to what lies beyond this life and most of them contain some kind of plan for redemption. Many religions claim you can earn your way to heaven. The only exception to this is found in Christianity. It is only through Jesus Christ that a soul can find redemption. It's only by God's grace! Only through Jesus can sins be forgiven and salvation secured. You can't earn salvation through good works, or buy it, or do anything to deserve it! No single life in the history of humanity has had a more significant impact than that of the Lord Jesus Christ. If all roads lead to heaven, why would God send His Son into the world to die as the sacrifice for sin? It would make no sense for God to make that kind of a sacrifice if there were other ways to find salvation.

"For God so loved the world that He gave His only begotten Son, that whoever believes in Him shall not perish, but have eternal life." John 3:16 NASB

I recently had an experience that provided great insight into the extent of God's love for mankind. Both of my sons have taken up the sport of big game hunting, with elk being their preferred game to hunt. Well, in the process of them getting involved in the sport, they renewed my interest in the sport, inviting me to tag along whenever possible. My youngest son, Dennis, has really taken to the sport of archery hunting. Which of course, is really much more of a sport. It's probably one of the most difficult of any type of hunting. Now, to me, the best part of hunting is getting out in the middle of God's creation to enjoy nature at its very best.

Dennis was shown a premium hunting area by my longest and closest friend Jerry. We had been hunting this particular area for several days, seeing mature bull elk every day of the season. We just hadn't gotten quite close enough to get off a shot. Once again, we had made our way up the extreme 4-wheel drive road on our ATVs nearly an hour before sunrise. We discovered this one area at the top of the ridge where the elk continued to come out of the trees to cross the meadow toward the dark timber. We strategically positioned ourselves in order to have the best chance to catch the elk crossing a small meadow. Dennis positioned himself at the bottom edge of the meadow along a trail's edge in a natural bowl. I found a place at the edge of an aspen grove near the top of the meadow that allowed me to have an unrestricted view across the meadow.

After getting in position, we settled in, waiting for the sun to rise while nestling in to the camouflaged, natural cover. One of the challenges of archery hunting is learning how to blend in to the surroundings in order to get close enough to the game to get a shot. Sixty- to seventy yards is probably one of the longest shots that most hunters would feel comfortable trying to make. I found a place to sit in the aspen grove that really allowed me to be out of sight, while allowing me an excellent vantage point. As the sun began to peek above the jagged mountain silhouette in the east, the birds began to chirp around me, while several elk began bugling just a few hundred yards away from our position. Sitting there in total silence, I had my compound bow resting on my crossed legs, with an arrow nocked in place. I had my arms resting on the bow with every inch of my body covered in camouflage outerwear, even my hands. The only part of me not concealed by the "camo" were my eyes which were exposed by the narrow slit in my head cover.

When the sun was completely exposed above the horizon, with brilliant rays of sunlight engulfing me, I silently sat in my camouflaged attire. Several sparrows flew into the branches of my cover with one landing on my hand, eyeballing me for nearly a minute before realizing I was an unnatural part of the landscape. It was quite an experience to have my identity concealed to even the birds, making me feel like I really was almost one with nature. Sitting there, I began to hear a bull elk huffing and snorting in the trees just below me. I quietly stood up in the aspen, in order to get a better look around while positioning myself for a shot if the elk came my way. I stood there for probably twenty minutes, listening to the elk moving closer to me with his grunts and snorts getting louder by the minute. In the distance from across the meadow, several other elk continued to bugle with their challenging call.

Suddenly, from across the meadow, I heard something come crashing through the dark timber toward me. I turned to face the charging onslaught, which sounded like a large herd of elk barreling through the downed timber in the dense forest. The crashing quickly got louder, and closer to the edge of the meadow. I double checked my arrow to make sure it was properly nocked on the string, slowly pulling my bow up to a position, ready to draw. My heart nearly jumped out of my chest when the animal broke through the trees into the meadow. It wasn't an elk at all, but instead it was a gigantic black mama bear, with her cub running close behind in her tracks. Actually, even though she was a black bear by breed, she was a beautiful shade of cinnamon. At forty yards away, she stopped dead in her tracks, to stand up on her hind legs. I swear that she must have been at least seven-feet tall while standing on her hind legs. It was obvious that she was ready for winter as she looked enormous. I bet she weighed close to four-hundred pounds. She was staring straight at me, but I couldn't tell if she could see me, or smell me, or just sense me.

While still holding my bow in one hand, I reached down to pull out my 9mm Ruger pistol. In an instant, I realized that my 9mm with its eight-shot capabilities was probably just going to make mama bear mad at me if it came to a confrontation. I remember whispering, "Jesus, help me!" as the bear continued to stare at what seemed to be directly at me. Suddenly, the yearling cub ran back into the woods behind its mama, causing the big bear to follow it back into the trees. I sighed a deep sigh of relief, thinking that I had dodged a bullet. Suddenly, I realized that Dennis was somewhere down in the trees not far from where the bears had headed. Those bears couldn't have been more than twenty yards back in the trees when the most ferocious and death-defying sounds I've ever heard completely swallowed the serenity of that peaceful mountainside.

The sounds that came out of the trees sounded like something out of Jurassic park. They were the most gruesome, terrifying, horrific sounds I had ever heard. I could hear the bear roaring as it attacked something. I heard screams that sounded almost human. It sounded like the bear was attacking my son. With an adrenaline rush like I've never experienced before in my life, I bolted across the meadow with a frenzied terror, bow and arrow in one hand, my 9mm pistol in the other. I was on a dead run toward the trees, straight toward the raging battle that was going on in the dark timber. The bear attack continued as I approached the edge of the trees. In a determined panic, I let out a thunderous battle cry, "Dennnnis . . ." I screamed at the top of my lungs as loud as possible as I continued my terror-induced sprint.

"Daaaad . . ." Dennis yelled out as he came tearing up the trail from the bottom of the meadow. I was never so relieved to hear my son as we met at the very edge of the meadow.

"What, did you get an elk?" he excitedly asked.

"No, it was a mama bear!" I exclaimed. "It attacked something in the woods" I blurted out as I tried to catch my breath. "I thought it was you!" I exclaimed with tears building in my eyes.

It took nearly two hours for the adrenaline induced trembling to subside, and my heart to slow to a normal rate. Never have I experienced such terror. We weren't sure what the bear attacked, but I think it might have been a male bear, attacking the cub before mama intervened. We had seen a huge male black bear in the area a few days earlier, and they have been known to attack a cub if it isn't its own. The battle was probably between the sow and the boar, as the yearling cub screamed out with a near-human squeal.

As I slowly gathered my composure, with the event continuously rewinding through my mind like a terror-filled nightmare, I realized that God must have felt the same way as His Son came to this Earth to die on the cross for the salvation of mankind. God willingly sent Jesus to this world, to live as one of us, to suffer and die on the cross as the sacrifice for our sin. Jesus willingly died for us while God stood by to watch. Jesus came to this world to be fed to the bears. That's how much God loves you and me! He loves us unconditionally! He was willing to do whatever it would take to allow us to come back into fellowship with Him. The Creator died for our sin. "No one has greater love than this, that someone would lay down his life for his friends," (John 15:13 HCSB), which is exactly what Jesus did for us, because of His love for His creation.

Most scholars agree that Jesus was a historical figure; a man that lived nearly two thousand years ago in a small little region in the Mideast known as Galilee. Many religions recognize him as a notable teacher, a rabbi, a prophet and/or a man of God. But really, who is Jesus? Jesus is not an expression of exasperation, a word of profanity or vulgarity—just the opposite. Jesus is the *name above all names*. He is the *King of kings* and *the Lord of lords*. He is the *Alpha and the Omega, the beginning and the end*!

Jesus is more than just some historical figure. He has inspired more songs, been the subject of more books, has stirred the hearts of more poets, and roused the talents of more artists than any other person in the history of the world. Why, it's because of Who He Is! Jesus is *the Author and the Finisher of our faith*! "Therefore we also, since we are surrounded by so great a cloud of witnesses, let us lay aside every weight, and the sin which so easily ensnares us, and let us run with endurance the race that is set before us, looking unto Jesus, the author and finisher of our faith, who for the joy that was set before Him endured the cross, despising the shame, and has set down at the right hand of the throne of God" (Hebrews 12:1, 2 NKJV).

The earliest memories of my life intertwine with going to church and learning about Jesus. I was blessed to grow up in a home that placed Christ at its center and made church an active part of life. Looking back I could compare our family to the television family from "*Leave it to Beaver*, the "Cleavers," with the exception we had three boys in the house rather than just Wally and the Beaver. Growing up, I never had a doubt in my mind about the love Jesus had for me. I knew beyond a shadow of a doubt that Jesus was real, that He was the Son of God, born of a virgin. He lived a sinless life, and died an excruciating death on the cross for my sins. On the third day He rose from the grave and lives forever more. Jesus offers the free gift of life everlasting if you only choose to believe.

In our home, Jesus was significant. We prayed before every meal, and around the dinner table we discussed the Bible and faith. We attended church services every week. As a teenager, after being immersed in the Christian faith, I accepted Jesus into my heart and I made the decision to follow after Him all the days of my life. My life was changed forever! What I learned through my childhood is that "experiencing Jesus isn't an event that happens at church on Sunday, it's a lifestyle."

I have had people imply that the only reason I'm a Christian is because I was brainwashed from my youth. I follow Jesus, because I have personally experienced His love and throughout my life, I have seen His faithfulness and grace in action. Nobody has changed the world like Jesus, His birth is so significant that it split recorded history into two parts: AD—Anno Domini and BC—Before Christ. Philip Yancey's book, *The Jesus I Never Knew*, summarizes the true essence of the mystery of Jesus this way: "I am drawn to Jesus, irresistibly, because He positioned himself as the dividing point of life—my life." For 2000 years, the influence Jesus had on the lives of people has never been surpassed. People who encounter the risen Christ are totally transformed.

My life is a witness to this proclamation. It started as a child, being raised in a family of faith. My journey took me to a mountainside in the Rocky Mountains of Colorado where I had my first personal encounter with Jesus. I have traveled along the living waters of the gently flowing streams of faith. At times, I found myself in the desert, but before long, I found an oasis that provided comfort and respite from the harsh elements of life. At times I traveled through the valley of the shadow of death, as well as through the green pastures of life. My journey continues today as I strive to serve the Lord and Master, the One I chose to follow more than forty years ago. One day, this journey of life will culminate when my time comes to "take the wings of the dawn!" I know I will be ready, I made my reservation a long time ago.

I have often heard stories about people's experiences of a loved one passing from this world into the next. So many times, those stories include descriptions of the person lifting their hand toward the ceiling reaching out to touch the hand of their Savior. That's exactly what Tim did, and I was a witness to my friend Mary doing the same. As you close your eyes in death, you will find yourself standing in the presence of Jesus; that is if you have accepted Him as the Lord and Master of your life; if you made the decision to follow after Him. In 2 Corinthians 5:8 NKJV, the Apostle Paul tells Christians, "To be absent from the body and to be present with the Lord."

Death is not the end of our journey. Jesus has given us a promise. He said, "In my Father's house are many mansions: if it were not so, I would have told you. I go to prepare a place for you. And if I go and prepare a place for you, I will come again and receive you unto myself, that where I am, there you may be also" (John 14:2, 3 NKJV).

When your time comes, and there is no doubt that it will come, will you be ready to go? As I stated earlier, the reality of life in this world is that it is temporary—finite, it has a beginning and it has an end. At this very moment you are encountering the *dash* between the dates of your earthly existence. Do you know what lies beyond this world? Your soul will continue on when you depart from this world and there are only two options for where you will spend your eternity— heaven or hell? When you take your final breath of the Earth's atmosphere, will you "take the wings of the dawn" or will you tumble into the "eternal abyss of darkness," where you will be completely and totally separated from the grace and mercy of God, or anything that is pleasant or good? Do you know where you will spend eternity? The options are limited. If you know Jesus—if you have asked Him into your heart—if you believe that He is the Son of God Who died for your sins, and Who rose from the grave—you will "take the wings of the dawn." You will spend eternity in the heavenly paradise of God's presence! "Jesus said to him, 'I am the way, and the truth, and the life; no one comes to the Father but through Me'" (John 14:6).

Jesus has done everything He can to ensure your eternal destiny, but it does require you to make a conscious choice. Will you let Him into your heart? Will you choose to follow after Him all the days of your life? Don't allow Deadly Sin Number Seven, "Living a life in denial of God," to determine your eternal destination. There is no greater question to answer than the one that determines your eternal destiny. The choice—your destiny is entirely up to you! Tim and I made our reservations more than forty years ago. Tim was ready to reach out to take the hand of Jesus when his time came. I pray that you, too, will be ready when your day arrives.

Then when "the last enemy that shall be destroyed is death," I Corinthians 15:26 NKJV, we "shall mount up on wings as eagles," we "shall run and not be weary," we "shall walk and not faint," (Isaiah 40:31 NKJV).

Only through Jesus, our Maker, Creator, Savior and Lord, we too shall one day take the "wings of the dawn," and so we shall be with our Lord, forever and ever! Amen.

The sun does rise, the sun does set, the moon shines bright at night;
God saw the "day" that He had made, and knew that it was right . . .
"Day" is done and all is well, the sting of death is past,
We'll reign with Him in heaven, Perfect unity . . . at last!

—Clarice D. Cook

"Buddies Forever"

The sun does rise, the sun does set,
the moon shines bright at night;
God saw the "day" that He had made,
and knew that it was right . . .
Pre-dawn days, Creation days,
days born of time and space;
Earth's great wonders came to be,
Through God's abounding grace.
Days of birth, genetic days,
rich heritage displayed;
God breathes sweet life into each soul,
great men this way are made.
Trail-crossed days, Kismet days,
days of destinies,
The lives of many people,
determine family trees.
Days of yore, days long past,
In retrospect we see,
That trails of many distant paths,
created you and me.
Paths emerged from long ago;
but who and what we are,
Depends on fate of days now gone,
and what's written in each star.
Days in the lives of new-born babes,
Will span the gulf of time,
Soul-searching days, goal reaching days,
bring days of heights sublime.
Those days of long past heritage,
breathe life into each soul,
Days of purpose to each life born,
brings time to reach "the goal."
"The goal" in life, "The goal" in death,
our days are numbered here;
"A time to live, a time to die,"
our God is always near!

The sun does rise, the sun does set,
the moon shines bright at night;
God saw the "day" that He had made,
and knew that it was right . . .
Childhood days, carefree days,
Days filled full of joy,
Days enmeshed by time and space,
in the lives of two small boys.
Summer days, winter days,
spring and autumn, too;
Each and every day o'er flowed,
with all the things to do!
From baby days to manhood,
the days were filled with fun;
No day was ever wasted,
No day was really done.
Laughter, shouts and giggles,
Echoed through the air;
Conspirators in action,
the world was theirs to share.
From rattles, balls and baby things,
to trikes and bikes and skis,
Fishin' poles and golfin' gear
—they had a need of these.
Days of playful pretense,
when stories come alive,
Cowboys, Indians, Pirate games,
how did these boys survive?
"Robin Hood" and "Big John" too,
spent hours in the woods,
Along with all the "Merry Men,"
they shared their borrowed goods.
Days of unknown artistry,
when "Van Goghs" shine and bloom;
Fame can soon become short-lived,
with a mother's voice of doom!

"Up de lazy riber" days,
    Emprise as "Tom" and "Huck,"
"We'll get this raft a floatin',
    with just a little luck."
These were the famous "whitewash kids,"
    In days of long ago,
Were they dressed in Sunday best,
    did their painting bring them woe?
Learning days, growing days,
    Time comes to go to school,
The "lesson" learned in early life,
    Is to "Follow every Rule . . . "

The sun does rise, the sun does set,
    the moon shines bright at night;
God saw the "day" that He had made,
    and knew that it was right . . .
Magical days, mystical days,
    hours filled with fun,
Water sports and rivalries,
    reflections in the sun.
Camping days, skiing days,
    days lived on the lake,
Boating, fishing, swimming,
    a great childhood this does make!
Happy days, sun-drenched days,
    exploring nature's joys,
Days of roaming o'er the hills,
    proclaim the ways of boys.
Mountains, lakes and rivers,
    all playgrounds wonderful,
Yet always special to the heart,
    was Grandpa's fishin' hole.
Blissful days together,
    finding treasures by the droves:
An Indian piece, a pretty rock,
    lacy sea shells in the coves.

Horny toads and pollywogs,
and lots of other things;
Rattles from a rattlesnake,
gossamer butterfly wings.
Days of finding things to do,
"I'll race you back and then,
We'll gather eggs for Grandma,
Chase the chickens 'round the pen."
Lazy days, leisure days,
day dreams may come true;
Each day is greeted with a grin,
there is so much to do!
Vacation days, Lake Powell days,
the high-light of July,
Majestic scenes, breathtaking sights,
beneath the deep blue sky.
Exploring days, fast-paced days,
with never enough time,
The days pass by too quickly,
pleasure reaches heights sublime.
Days of close togetherness,
enwrapped in "family love,"
A boyhood life of happiness,
a blessing from above . . .

The sun does rise, the sun does set,
the moon shines bright at night;
God saw the "day" that He had made,
and knew that it was right . . .
Church camp days and Bible days,
to learn of Jesus love:
Blessed days, Holy days,
faith cometh from above.
Fun-filled days, exciting days,
days of high adventure;
Quiet days, thoughtful days,
with visions of the future.

Romantic days, first love days,
thrill to that gentle kiss;
Moonlight walks, sweetheart talks,
memories are made of this.
Red-faced days of embarrassment,
a trait among the youth,
Time to find a place to run,
and hide the awful truth.
Days to heed God's message,
convictions draweth nigh,
The Holy Ghost is speaking;
turn not your face awry.
Days of choice, commitment days,
which path in life to take;
Once faith takes root in your soul,
you know which choice to make.
Christian days, faith-filled days,
of devotion, worship, prayer,
Reaching out to others,
God's Holy Word to share.
Caring Days, sharing days,
when lives become entwined,
The joys of shared togetherness,
two souls will tightly bind.
All these days together,
make up the world of boys;
The sad day falls so quickly
—Time to put away the toys . . .

The sun does rise, the sun does set,
the moon shines bright at night;
God saw the "day" that He had made,
and knew that it was right . . .
Memories days, nostalgic days,
days when one must ponder,
Of times now past, days long gone,
"What is this life?" we wonder . . .

Shocking days, Denial days,
    what fate life holds in store;
The heart cries out in agony,
    reaching deep within its core.
Days of anger, unbelief,
    grasping out at straws,
Seeking for the "answers,"
    searching for the cause.
Days of hurt and stress-filled days,
    the soul sinks, oh, so low,
Reach out to touch the hand of Him,
    Who shares our every woe.
Days of turning all to Him,
    Who knows our every need;
He sees the future from the past,
    "The Shepherd," He will lead.
"Not my will, but Thine alone,"
    This is the prayer we pray,
Grant us courage, strength and faith,
    to see us through the day.
Precious days, fragile days,
    Life is now—today,
Yesterday's gone, tomorrow not come,
    forever? A breath away.
Days of support, of reaching out,
    to draw all loved ones 'round,
To share the message of the "faith,"
    Greater love cannot be found.
Days of living close to God,
    'Mid miracles and dreams,
Affirming deep commitments,
    eternal peace it brings.
Final days together, in communion,
    rich and sweet;
Leaving footprints in the sand,
    'Til once again we meet.

Days of watching the setting sun,
    as the tears are softly flowing,
The final moment when day is done?
    There is no way of knowing . . .

The sun does rise, the sun does set,
    the moon shines bright at night;
God saw the "day" that He had made,
    and knew that it was right . . .
Cloudy days, sunless days,
    Stroke softly as a feather,
The Creator masks the sting of death,
    thru times of stormy weather,
Days of sorrow, days of woe,
    Days so filled with grief,
Days that rip the heart apart,
    to test your faith's belief.
Healing days, peace-filled days,
    the heart with time does mend,
As Jesus takes away the hurt;
    He is our dearest friend.
Welcome days of the morning dawn,
    after the wings take flight;
Dipping, diving, soaring high,
    pursuing His radiant light.
Future days, heavenly days,
    Time will never sever,
The tie that binds not just for life . . .
    There buddies dwell forever.
Eternal days, glorious days,
    where "day" fades back to space;
There He will draw His children home,
    and greet them face to face.
To live with Him Forever,
    In that home beyond the skies,
Rich days of true contentment,
    in that land of paradise!

The sun does rise, the sun does set,
    the moon shines bright at night;
God saw the "day" that He had made,
    and knew that it was right . . .
"Day" is done and all is well,
    the sting of death is past,
We'll reign with Him in heaven,
    Perfect unity . . . at last!

—Clarice D. Cook

Connect with the Author:

Email: IHSPublishing@yahoo.com
Website: www.IHSPublishing.com